Heart to Heart Selling

"This is a wonderful book that provides you with the inside knowledge and understanding that will enable you to sell more, easier than ever before."

- **Brian Tracy**, author, Ultimate Sales Success

"Cezar wants to inspire you to explore the paradigm of selling that highly successful salespersons are living up to. You'll discover how to make an impact on your clients, not through intricate techniques or manipulation tactics, but by having your inner values aligned and congruent with your actions, by influencing without constricting, by allowing without neediness, by offering value from a place of presence and connection."

- **Christy Whitman**, New York Times Bestselling Author, CEO and Founder of The Quantum Success Coaching Academy, www.christywhitman.com

"There is a misunderstanding about what selling means, and that's why many salespersons and business owners are distancing themselves from this concept. Cezar proposes a fascinating paradigm for selling and, if we were to adopt it, selling becomes a joyful, spiritual, respectable and profitable activity, for everyone involved."

- **Rachael Jayne Groover**, Author of Powerful and Feminine, Creator of the *Art of Feminine Presence* TM

"Heart to Heart Selling is the first sales book I have read that truly digs into the sales experience, allowing the reader to improve their own selling habits. Cezar Cehan unravels the history and psychology behind selling while offering alternative strategies. He utilizes examples from his extensive experience in hypnotherapy that enable the reader to relate from a personal level rather than someone else's reality that may be from a different industry or generation. I would recommend Heart to Heart Selling to anyone working in sales. Be sure to bring an open mind."

> - **David Scott**, Director of Sales, *Embassy Suites Omaha-La Vista, Nebraska, USA*

"Cezar shares a unique perspective on selling and how to awaken your natural ability to sell no matter what level of sales experience you have. This book is a <u>must read</u> for anyone who wants to sell a product or service and feel good about asking for the money and congruently collecting it."

> - **Amir Mahmoud**, *www.BusinessAndMarketingMentors.com*

"There are hundreds of books covering all kinds of selling skills. And then you find a diamond called Cezar Cehan and his book called "Heart to Heart Selling" and you realize that this is the missing piece to this big jigsaw puzzle called "selling". Heart to Heart Selling goes beyond all these traditional sales books. It brings to your awareness the human side of selling. This is a book that you won't be able to put away. You will get back to it. It has exercises to help you have an experience of how to Become a salesperson of artistry."

> - **Andreas Dorn**, Certified NLP Trainer, Master Trainer of Hypnosis, Asia Mind Dynamics (Malaysia, Southeast Asia), www.AsiaMindDynamics.com, "Creating Change That Lasts"

"I always considered my high school and University colleague as a very intelligent and innovative person. Despite this, reading this book was really surprising. It's a very interesting approach of the selling process. I consider it very useful for my activity as a business consultant and also for all the businesspersons who, in a way or another, are involved in selling products or services. I might say with the author's words that he didn't convince me to read the entire book but this book came from his heart to my heart."

- **Iulian Warter**, Partner, Consulting Experts-Warter, Romania

"I really enjoyed reading this book. It was a very pleasant reading and it offered a new and interesting perspective on selling. I must especially remark the "engineering" approach which led to an alternative model of selling, focusing on the exchange of value.

I recommend this book to all the salespersons, no matter from which national, professional and organizational culture they are coming from. More than that, I consider this book interesting for business owners from various fields."

- **Liviu Warter**, Partner, Consulting Experts-Warter, Romania

"My reaction is "Wow!" It's a different type of selling manual. A different perspective over the salesperson-client relationship. In a world so recklessly mad about reaching selling targets it's almost unconceivable – however, not impossible – that such relationship could be based on trust, connection and true partnership; that the client can feel safe and secure that the salesperson will honestly take care of him; that the interaction is not just for 'making a sale', but for a long term connection."

"Great book! I would prefer all of our salespeople use H2H method vs the traditional sales methods in practice today. I can see how this would shift the selling paradigm we are holding today. I found the book to be very enlightening, putting a lot of things into perspective about why we look at salespeople the way we do. It also helped me understand why I enjoy selling even though I never wanted to be a salesman. I really enjoy building relationships with people. The book also reinforced the belief that I have that value is relevant to each individual. We can't make someone see value in our product/service/organization, they need to see value in it for themselves."

I was always convinced that I have nothing to do with selling. However, reading your book I realized that my entire activity is based on selling/buying process: the presentation of a project is actually selling ideas, a job application is selling of knowledge. "Heart to heart selling" is not an arid manual of selling techniques nor a romantic book as the title may suggest, but for me is a book that precisely makes an introspection in our hearts, makes us knowing better our inside and reveals things that we do on a daily basis without the conscience that we really do it. We sell objects, values, ideas, feelings... and, when we sell from heart to heart, from connection, it feels so much better for everybody involved.

"You have in your hands a very special book. Cezar Cehan has created a paradigm shift with his book *Heart to Heart Selling.* This book is required reading for anyone who calls themselves a salesman or anyone who is planning on buying something in the future. *Heart to Heart Selling* lifts the proverbial fog from an activity in which we all engage and gets down to what is truly important inside of that interaction. It is guaranteed to change the way you think and feel about one of the most fundamental processes in our society."

> - **Rick Harman**, CH - Educator and internationally certified hypnotist

"I have often disagreed with traditional sales methods and have successfully grown our businesses based on building strong relationships and offering our friends and clients a fair exchange of value without applying any form of coercion, deception or closing techniques.

Heart to Heart Selling by Cezar Cehan provides a fresh and professional perspective on the art and philosophy of selling. With many nuggets of golden wisdom in these pages, this book offers a very fair exchange of value."

> - **Jules A. Lalonde,** MBA CFP CLU CHFS, Director of Wealth Management, Greenvale Group Advisors Inc., Sudbury, ON, Canada

"Cezar, thank you! This could be the most powerful book in sales that I've ever read. It has resolved the inner conflict between my moral beliefs and all the "sales tactics" I've learned over the years. Heart to Heart Selling will definitely change how I approach and teach the sales process. I feel excited to master this philosophy of selling and share it with the world.

P.S. I started reading Heart to Heart Selling yesterday, I'm starting it the second time today."

   - **Patrick Bohn**, Professional Salesman and Success Coach

"*Heart to Heart Selling* is a great pragmatic book of ethics and adds a new dimension to the art of selling as a profession. Cezar is the author that makes the connection between the seller and the buyer, bringing selling into the best approach for both parts. We buy because we need the item or service we buy. The seller sells with pleasure an item when the buyer truly needs it. It is maybe in the human nature to do useful things and activities, so selling from heart to heart is a simple natural thing that is many times ignored."

   - **Doina Platon**, Continuous Education Director at "APOLLONIA" University from Iasi

"In *Heart to Heart Selling,* Cezar presents a new paradigm for influence. Interestingly enough, any successful communicator, salesperson, or influencer already lives out these principles in their life knowing it or not. The principles in this book are so powerful and can create a tremendous impact in your life. The ideas in Heart to Heart Selling will help you to improve your communication with others, your relationships, and your results in life. Even if you do not want to become a world class salesman, pick up this book to help transform your relationships."

   - **Shawn Schweier**, www.the-irresistible-man.com

Heart to Heart Selling

Create clients through nurturing Connection

Cezar Cehan

www.hearttoheartselling.com

Heart to Heart Selling

Note: In order to avoid the awkward "he/ she", "him/ her"
references, I chose to use the plural/ neutral "they" or "them"
even when referring to singular antecedents such as "person",
even though this construction is not entirely grammatically
correct.

Contact the author:
www.hearttoheartselling.com

ISBN-13: 978-1512104417
ISBN-10: 1512104418

First Edition

*To all of my mentors, trainers and friends –
too many to mention,
because they made me what I am today.*

*Many thanks to those who accepted my
formal and informal interviews and answered
honestly to my (unusual and often
uncomfortable) inquiries.*

Table of Contents

Author's Note

For the last few years I worked as a hypnotherapist, assisting people to quit smoking or to control their weight. At one moment, it occurred to me that the hypnosis session was, in fact, a sales interaction, in and of itself – although inverted: it was *the client* who asked me to "sell" them on the idea of not smoking anymore, and they even paid me in advance for that.

Yet, even if *they* were coming to me asking "to be sold", some of them would buy (i.e., would quit smoking), and others won't!

It was intriguing. I put on my thinking hat and I looked back at what happened in those sessions. I realized that the successful clients engaged wholeheartedly with the process/ the ritual that I was suggesting. The ones that didn't quit smoking held back and only superficially went through the motions.

Thus, my first conclusion was that *they* were the culprit: *they* didn't engage, see? But it didn't really feel complete, so I decided to step back furthermore and take an even larger perspective.

I noticed that, when the client engaged wholeheartedly with me, <I> was always *present, connected* with myself... no matter what the client did or said, I remained *present* and *connected* and I maintained a *playful* attitude, *non-attached* to the outcome, carrying no need to *prove* myself. In other words, the entire interaction was 'about them', nothing 'about me'. It was as like I didn't matter.

On another hand, *most* of the times when the client wasn't successful, <I> wasn't fully *present* and *connected* with myself: perhaps I carried some irritation from my personal life, or perhaps my Ego reacted to something they said or did, and I popped out of my Presence, or perhaps I wanted for them to be successful more than they wanted it, or perhaps I fell into a need to *prove* that I am good at what I do... Whatever it was, once my *presence* became unsteady, the interaction became 'about me', not anymore 'about them'.

My final conclusion is this: when my *presence* was hollow, the client felt that I wasn't there 'for them', but mostly 'for me', they felt that I was holding back, keeping my defenses up, having an ulterior motive. As a result, they didn't feel *safe and secure* in my presence, enough to allow themselves to abandon themselves in the process, to become *present* and to fully *engage* with the experiences I was trying to facilitate for them.

However, when I was committed to my own *presence* and *connection* to myself, regardless of how they responded, when I remained *playful* and *non-attached*, dropping any *need* to prove anything, they eventually sensed that I am there 'for them', vulnerable and true. This encouraged them to trust me, to allow themselves to become *present* on their own and to accept my invitation to *dance* and *play*. That's *connection*.

An important point is to realize that you cannot 'force' your *connection* to somebody – all you can do is open the door and invite them in. It starts with you 'going first': <you> first connect with yourself. When you talk to somebody from that place of *presence* and *connection* with yourself, you're actually talking to their 'true self', increasing the <u>probability</u> that their 'true self' will then grow stronger and stronger in their awareness. Since you show up vulnerable, open, not needing anything 'from them', but rather wanting something 'for them' (and only to the extent that they decide to accept it, respecting their freedom to choose whatever they want to do) – this increases the probability that they will feel safe and secure with you, enough to relax, to loosen up their defenses and eventually to accept your invitation to *play* and *dance.*

It's almost like falling in love, really. "You can't hurry love", the song goes, and we all know it's true:

You can't hurry love
No, you'll just have to wait
She said love don't come easy
But it's a game of give and take
You can't hurry love
No, you'll just have to wait
Just trust in a good time
No matter how long it takes

Why Did I Write this Book?

*"If you change the way you look at things,
the things you look at change."*
Wayne Dyer

What's the problem that this book aims to solve? Is this yet another book about selling techniques and marketing strategies, with tips and tricks on how to make people buy your stuff?

Not really.

It's about something better than that.

Why did I write it? What triggered my "compulsion" to write this message? Well, I stopped for a moment to pay attention to my experience of reality and I had some realizations, such as:

My therapy business was struggling because I could not sell my services with the same effectiveness that I had selling commodities for more than 20 years. Somehow, I felt like a fraud asking money for something that I loved doing and which was easy for me to do. Moreover, I realized that the vast majority of the therapists, coaches and even physicians (surprisingly, I know!) were in the same slump.

Business owners having a good product would not actively promote it, out of aversion of being labeled as "salespersons".

Friends confessed to me that they could never "be in selling", because selling seemed demeaning to them. Paradoxically, they also agreed that a society lacking selling and buying would soon dry and die.

Can you believe that quite a few business owners and salespersons declared that they resent talking to a salesperson?!

I've talked with salespersons that were genuinely uncomfortable with the paradigms of "making people buy", "handling objections" or using scripts designed to "persuade".

I've talked with salespersons dreading the activity of prospecting.

I've talked with salespersons who told me that they were perfectly fine presenting their product, but they could not ask the prospect for the buying agreement. They feared asking for money.

I've talked with salespersons who deeply believed that selling is about "convincing" or "persuading" people to buy their products. They considered it natural to use "deceiving" tools in the process. Their metaphor for selling was "a battle in which one wins".

I've talked with salespersons who were financially successful, but felt lack of integrity, they were stressed and divided inside and that prevented them from thriving.

I've met only a few who could honestly find selling as fun, enjoyable and fulfilling.

Aside from these symptoms everything was fine.

Only it was not.

I couldn't make sense of what was going on. So I put on my "coaching hat" and I started to ask questions. I interviewed many salespersons, business owners and also clients, on the "receiver" end of the process. The revelation that I had was that the struggling salespersons (me included) operated from a confused understanding of *what selling is* and *what* they were actually selling. The more I extended my research, the more I found the same evidence.

We Always Act in Coherence with Our Understanding of 'What Is'

Stephen R. Covey wrote "The way we see the problem is the problem."

Think of this for a moment...

Imagine there was a city where Green light meant Stop and Red light meant Go. If you were to drive through that city, you'd experience a lot of frustration. Nothing would work right for you, although you are doing everything right... according to *your understanding* of the traffic lights. There's nothing wrong with you or with your behavior, per se; only with the *meaning* you hold for the traffic lights.

Just for a moment, notice what happens within you as you read these statements:

"You have a valuable product and everybody needs it, so you have to convince people to buy it."

Can you sense how the second part is contradictory to the first part?

"Selling means to persuade or induce someone to buy... selling is about creating relationships."

Both sentences are culturally used to describe selling. Can you see how one excludes the other?

The contradictions are subtle and that's exactly what makes them powerful.

Considering how vague and double-binding the cultural understandings of this concept actually are, it's only to be expected that people would manifest such contradictory emotions about selling.

As an engineer, I wanted to find a solution. Thus, I dug deeper and I found that the concept of selling has been used for thousands of years. Originally it had a curious meaning: "to give", "to offer", "to sacrifice" and it was frequently used in religious contexts. There was no "convincing" and no "persuasion" connected with this concept, whatsoever. In other words, selling today is an activity that has nothing to do with its original meaning!

Selling Is Necessary

Going even deeper I found why selling is vital for the survival of any community: selling facilitates the **exchange of value**, and value can only grow when it is exchanged with another value. When value doesn't grow, it diminishes.

Coming back to "creating relationships" – a valuable relationship cannot be "created" or "built", but it only **emerges** between two people when each of them has the wellness of the other as primary focus. Think of any relationship in your life that you appreciate dearly and notice that this is the case. That means that you cannot meet the other person thinking "what do I get **from** you", but, above all, "what can I bring **for** you".

Interestingly enough, when interviewing successful salespersons, I discovered that they already view selling this way and operate from this perspective. So, I put together the pieces I collected from them, I connected them with the findings from etymology, I secured them with my understanding of how mind works and I built a scaffold for what I called "Heart to Heart Selling" (or short, "H2H Selling").

Why "Heart to Heart"

Why "Heart to Heart"? The magnetic and electrical fields produced by our heart are thousands of times stronger than the fields created by our brain. The quality of those fields are given by the quality of our emotions and of the feelings that we entertain in our heart. When we feel good about what we do, when we are joyful, present, connected and willing to serve others, then the way those fields will affect the matter they touch will create a reality of joy, connectedness and satisfaction.

Perhaps that's why Aristotle said that "Educating the mind without educating the heart is no education at all."

Now, I am not asking you to accept these ideas just yet; we'll discuss them in the next pages: not to convince you of the "rightfulness" of what I say, but to invite you to look at selling from a new perspective and notice what kind of difference does that make for you.

For instance, if you were to imagine thinking from the perspective I just painted above, what would be different in the way you sell? If your job was only to "offer" your product with no need to "make them buy", would you find it more enjoyable? If your purpose was to make sure **if** your product is, indeed, valuable to your prospect – instead of "convincing" them that it is – would you feel more at ease to ask questions and discuss your product with them?

What Is the Purpose of This Book

The purpose of this book is to propose an alternative model of selling, one which is elegant and respectable, enjoyable and effective, focusing on the exchange of value. If the current cultural paradigm about selling is disempowering and unethical for you or if it hinders your success, you are free to play and experiment with the "Heart to Heart (H2H) Selling" model explained in this book.

When selling from this perspective, you are able to wholeheartedly offer your product or service because your purpose is no longer to "make them buy", not even to "make a sale". Your purpose now is to *offer value* to your clients in a way that they are happy to buy it from you. When such a relationship of trust is allowed to emerge, they will want to do business with you again and again; moreover, they will bring their friends along since you proved you can be trusted.

Once you realize that selling and buying are not about "money", but about exchange of value, it's easy to shift your focus and attention (and the client's, as well) on the things that matter, like "what is the value that my prospect receives out of this?"

It's refreshing to sell when there's no need for "convincing" or "persuasion" tactics, "handling objections" or "justification for the price". When you sell by giving them an experience of a solution to their problem, they will feel the value of your offer, directly into their heart. Price is of a little importance. Value is the relevant thing.

It all becomes natural and flowing when you make the process "about them" and "about the value they receive", as it should be. The connection between you two grows all by itself when you are both present in the moment. There's no need to artificially "create a relationship".

My focus was to organize the material in this book as succinctly as possible. I took off what I considered redundant, without impairing the message. I wanted to keep here only the essential things. Thus, you should find it easy enough to refer back to certain ideas, if you need to refresh or clarify your mind. I also included a Glossary of Terms at the end of the book, to define some of the concepts that I used.

If you want to improve your selling effectiveness, you could continue to struggle learning more tactics and techniques in an attempt to cover up the turmoil underneath, the conflict within yourself.

Or, you can change it all from inside-out, building anew on a clean slate, allowing yourself to fall in love with this respectable profession of selling and feel proud creating value in your community.

We are influencing each other all the time, continuously, one way or another. We cannot escape that. Any act of influence is, in essence, an act of selling. Perhaps that's how the saying "everything is sales" emerged.

Albert Einstein said that "Peace cannot be kept by force; it can only be achieved by understanding." The purpose of this book is to bring peace between you and the selling process by proposing a different understanding about what selling is - not by teaching you more techniques so to force the results you want (although I will teach you techniques to facilitate that understanding).

When salespersons are genuinely focused on serving their clients, connecting with them at a deep level, this is bound to change people's view about the profession of selling, altogether. My higher purpose is that we shift the current cultural perspective and, by acting from a perspective of serving and connecting, we can bring *selling* to a respectable position – just as respectable as that of a physician, for instance. I don't see why not: both salespersons and physicians increase the value in their clients' lives.

The world will learn that selling is not about deceiving and that it can be beneficial, enjoyable and fun for all parties involved.

What Do I Want to Create

I believe that we are all already connected. We are not necessarily aware of this connection - because we're "thinking ourselves out of it" - and this is the reason why we treat each other as if we are separate, as obstacles between us and what we want.

But, what if we are here to actually serve each other in reaching what we want?

I want to live in a world where salespeople are no longer "pushing for the sale", a world where people are not "forcing" their own ideas and beliefs on others.

I want to live in a world where people are choosing to be friends with each other. Among friends there is an aura of trust, respect and consideration, and they are treating each other just the same as they would like to be treated themselves.

I want to live in a world where people are true to themselves and to each other, present and connected, candid and impartial about their desires, living in flow with the natural order of things.

This is not an utopia, and it's easier to actualize than it looks. All we need to do is change a little story in our heads, a distorted paradigm that creates this unpleasant slope. That story is "I NEED to make this sale" or "I NEED them to accept my idea" or even "I AM RIGHT and they are Wrong". This is a story created by our Ego, out of its own need for self-confirmation. Once we raise our levels of consciousness and understanding, and we allow ourselves to come from a place of wanting something FOR other people, instead of FROM them, that story would dissolve all by itself.

As a result, we will all allow ourselves to be present, true to each other and connected, living in a partnership on this planet, together for a common purpose: to realize that, ultimately, we are all coming from the same place.

CHAPTER 1:

Introduction

"Many people have asked me what my profession is. I've always said, and I'm proud to say it: <I am a salesman!>"
W. Clement Stone

I am a Salesman and I am proud to say that. Ever since I graduated college as a mechanical engineer, I created my own companies and I sold the products or services I was promoting. There are about 25 years since I started this journey and I don't regret a single moment of it.

During this time, I have read many books about selling, marketing and business and I trained with internationally recognized trainers. Given my education, I took an engineering perspective over the process of selling, attempting to identify why and how certain things work. Moreover, since selling is strongly connected with the human psychology, I studied and became certified as a Master Practitioner and a Trainer in Neuro Linguistic Programming, Hypnosis, Life Coaching and so on. Then I decided that my experience and skills would be much more useful for a better purpose: to serve people who want to deliberately create a passionate and meaningful life for themselves. In other words, I became a change-worker, a coach and a trainer.

And that's when my problems began...

The Huge Distinction between Selling Commodities and Selling Coaching or Therapy

You see, I had no problem selling a product that I knew would deliver the features for which it was purchased. I could test it and provide proof (both for the client and for myself) that – for instance - the alarm system will activate when triggered or that the auto mechanic will be able to replace the broken part. My belief in the product strengthened because of my ability to provide proofs, so I could easily sell it.

Things are entirely different in the change-work business. Here, I thought that the 'product' I was selling was 'the change' that the client wanted to produce. Keeping the same logic as above, in order to "sell it congruently" and to "strengthen my belief" in my 'product', it meant that I should be able to "prove" that 'the change' - that the client wanted - would manifest.

However, there is a huge distinction here that I failed to recognize for a long time: the alarm system would activate when triggered regardless of the client's input, whereas in the change-work, the client's role is of the essence. The auto mechanic would be able to replace the broken part because the car has no consciousness, no Ego and there is no such thing as the car's "resistance", "engagement" or "willingness to release the broken part".

Experienced change-workers know that they are teachers, influencers and that they are not able to "make" someone change, if that person doesn't want to change (perhaps I should not say that it is "impossible", but rather improbable and frustrating). Michael Perez said once (on doing change-work)... "I can stack the deck, but they've gotta pull a card for the magic to happen."

Once the client became an active part of the change-work success, things turned really frustrating for me – from the selling standpoint. Why is that? Well, if the client would not engage with the process, the transformation could not occur. It was a double bind. That meant that I could no longer guarantee the result for the client!

In other words, if my "product" was 'the change' that the client wanted, I could not bring "proofs" and guarantees that I can deliver it – neither to them, nor to myself. Subsequently, my belief in my "product" started to shake and – since I cannot successfully sell something I do not believe in – my sales fell.

I was frustrated because I could not understand what was happening. I used to be a great salesman, with great results and now I had started to think that something was wrong with me!

Looking around, though, I noticed that many therapists, hypnotists, coaches, even physicians, were having the same experience. They knew they were prepared, well trained and confident in their skills. However, when the time came to promote their service, they would become shy, vague and evasive. As a result, their business practice would not thrive.

A well-known forum for hypnotherapists ran an anonymous survey which revealed that most therapists, hypnotists or coaches make less than $15,000 per year from their therapy business. In other words, I wasn't alone in this puzzle and this could only mean that the issue had a deeper cause, which affected many people, in particular therapists, coaches and physicians – but not only...

Many sales representatives and business owners don't consider themselves as salespersons and refute the concept of selling. They try to convince everybody that they "don't sell anything" and many even state with pride "I hate selling". It is no wonder why their businesses were struggling.

The Misunderstanding Is Even Deeper

I looked deeper into this issue and I discovered that the concept of selling – in and of itself – is generally treated with disrespect in our society. As a result, many people don't want to be associated with selling or to be called "a salesperson". Actually, to call someone "a salesperson" is often used in a derogatory manner, as an insult. The profession of selling is regarded as not worthy of respect and as "something you do in between jobs", as Brian Tracy pointed out.

To be truthful to the end, there are reasons why this happens. I don't need to remind you of the selling "schemes" that ran around or about the "pushy" and "arrogant" salespersons who would do anything to "manipulate" people into buying whatever they sell. There is even a sense of pride among those salespersons to be able "to sell ice to an Eskimo".

I thought that the current model for selling was not helpful anymore – neither for the clients, nor for the salespersons - and that a new model could be useful. That means we need to shift our perspective about this concept altogether, to reconsider our understanding about 'what selling is' - NOT just to add more techniques and tricks, so to "convince" or "persuade" more people to buy our products...

If you can relate to my story so far, keep reading. You may be a "rookie" trying to adjust to the pressure that's common in this industry or a "veteran" that fights with the stress; or, perhaps you're doing great and the current paradigm handicaps you from turning your activity into artistry...

You're in the right place, because this book is about bringing a fresh perspective over the concept of selling, which will allow you to wholeheartedly talk about your passion to the people who might benefit from your expertise. In doing that, you'll foster beautiful relationships with your clients, from which everybody will win.

CHAPTER 2:

I Sell Commodities. Is this Book Only about Selling "Intangibles", as Coaching?

"All decisions are emotional in origin. [...] If we say that we are going to do this for logical reasons, it only means we have more emotion invested in that reason than we have in another reason."
Brian Tracy, Psychology of Selling

This is a great question: What is it that you're really selling?

It has been said that all decisions are emotional and I believe that. How is this affecting your selling style? Well, if you choose to focus solely on the *pragmatic* nature of the goods that you sell, without engaging any of their *emotional* side, you're only limiting the impact of your presentation.

Some people think that the nature of their business, of their clients or of the products they sell doesn't allow for bringing any emotions into the conversation. I know what you're referring to. However, I will show you how you can engage the client's emotions in a subtle and effective way – yet natural and harmonious, which will create pleasant selling experiences and to long lasting relationships. This is the way the great salespersons do it.

But, I agree, there are selling interactions that are more rigid and more pragmatic than others. I believe that there are 3 main reference considerations that differentiate the types of things (products/ services) that are sold and bought:

- Things that require *little to no* emotional involvement from the part of the client, in order for them to consider the purchase as valuable:

  o e.g., an airline buying a number of airplanes from the manufacturer or a contractor buying nails from a hardware store.

  o There are some [more or less] rigid and pre-established criteria that need to be precisely fulfilled, in order for the transaction to take place.

  o The *value* of the purchase is given *almost* exclusively by the proper functionality (according to the specifications) of the thing which was bought.

  o The evaluation of that *value* is made in a pragmatic, matter-of-fact, utilitarian manner.

  o However, even buying a screwdriver may involve an emotional component. Many contractors, I noticed, when choosing their tools, have preferences for one brand or another, although there is no *precise* reason for that.

- Things that require at least *some* emotional participation from the part of the client, in order for them to consider the purchase as valuable:

  o E.g., a car, a pair of shoes, a smartphone, etc.

  o Although the client has some criteria to satisfy, the overall satisfaction of the purchase still lies in their personal experience of the thing they bought.

- o The client's "likes" or "dislikes" are important factors in how they evaluate the purchase - the *value* they received out of buying that thing - and in the probability that they will buy again from you.

- Things that require *major* emotional engagement from the part of the client, in order for them to consider the purchase as valuable:

  - o E.g., therapy, coaching, medical services, etc.

  - o There is a highly personal interaction between the therapist and the client.

  - o If the client comes to the therapist's office with an attitude of disbelief, disengagement, rejection, expecting to "be convinced", then the personal change they are after is improbable to happen – thus, they get no value out of the transaction.

The things that people sell and buy are within a *continuum* along those three guidelines. There are no black-and-white boundaries. Also, those 'things' may very well change their position along this continuum, according to the dynamic that is running in that selling interaction.

The reason I brought this up is to emphasize that even when selling "practical goods", emotions are relevant. People make decisions based on emotions; so, connect with your client at a deeper level; go beyond the "benefits" and reach for the "meaning" that your client holds about that "practical good" and emphasize it, so that you increase the chances of them buying from you.

Considering the importance of the emotions in selling, the principles of "Heart to Heart (H2H) Selling" become essential for the client to have a powerful selling interaction and for them to experience the value of what you have to offer.

People don't buy "products"; they buy "states", "feelings", "meanings"... The classical theory says that people buy "benefits", but that concept is entirely rational and logical. I believe that people buy what those 'benefits' *mean* to them.

All decisions are emotional in nature. The sooner you realize this, the deeper the connection that you will create with your client and the higher their overall satisfaction.

CHAPTER 3:

How to Use this Book

"The greatest personal limitation is to be found not in the things you want to do and can't, but in the things you've never considered doing."
Richard Bandler, co-creator of Neuro Linguistic Programming

Think of this for a moment...

I am the cadet of my family. I have a brother who is several years older than me. As a child, I looked up to him and I wanted to be a "grown-up", as I saw him. However, I continued felling like a child – perhaps because, as I was growing older, he was also advancing in life, becoming more mature himself.

Now I realize that my mistake was that I was comparing myself *with him*, instead of evaluating *my own transformation* (i.e., the way I am "today" with how I was "yesterday"). In those times, I remember that I felt frustrated: I knew that becoming a "grown-up" was something that I was bound to become, it was in my very nature. Yet, I didn't feel that I was getting any closer to it, and I wanted it to happen NOW! I wanted those "benefits": to be taken more seriously, to be listened to, to 'be on my own'... I was 'needy' and I was trying to force things to happen – and, perhaps, that's exactly why they didn't!

I guess that one day I became exhausted of frustration and I *gave up the need* to be a grown-up. Instead, I remember that I started to *playfully pretend* that I was one. Before that, I would *strain* to appear something else than what I deeply felt I was - and, obviously, nobody took me seriously (which only augmented my frustration!). Now, I accepted that I was a child and I was simply *playing* with these new "pieces of behavior" that I copied from my brother. Strangely enough, the more I playfully "rehearsed" those behaviors, the more natural they became to me. The more natural they felt for me, the more 'congruent' I became and I noticed that people started to respond differently to me. Since I was playful and I wasn't *imposing* anything on others, they played back *with* me – willingly, voluntarily, because I gave them nothing to which to resist. I was getting the "perks" of a grown-up and I didn't even have to struggle for them; I was just playing.

That's how you shape your reality from Inside-Out.

The funny thing is that I was able to switch back and forth between the "child" and "grown-up" styles of behaving. My mind lived in some sort of "dual reality". I didn't have to cut-off the "child" part of me – I didn't want to, because I liked it, I enjoyed it and I still do. I believe that this was the real benefit of my "playfulness" strategy. I didn't replace one aspect of me with another one, but I became a "larger" person who incorporated both aspects.

That's what I would call 'expanding'.

Just Try It Out

As you read this book, I encourage you to loosen up your present beliefs and convictions about 'what selling is'. Put them aside, just for a while; I promise you, nobody will "steal" those beliefs from you. If you don't like what you read, you can always put them back.

Just for a while, be willing to play with a different perspective about this activity, be willing to explore and experiment with it, notice how it feels for you, notice what difference would that make – the same way you would try on a coat in the fitting room at the store: if you don't like it, then it's ok, you don't need to buy it; but at least you know.

However, if you *do* like it, please realize that this doesn't mean that you need to "forget" or "discard" everything you previously learned about selling. Not at all. My intention is to help you adopt a *congruent* way to **BE** when you are "doing" those techniques.

That "congruent way to BE" refers to having your inner values aligned with your outer actions and it is as important as the foundation is for a house. Even if you were to use the "tactics" and "techniques" that you learned in the past... when you *are coming* from a place of *connection* with your client, of *presence*, of *serving*, those techniques will **feel** differently to you and they will have a different impact on your client. It is just the same as the meaning of saying "I love you" or "Get out of here" changes, depending on your attitude and on your perspective when you say it.

Think of this for a moment...

Suppose your intention is to climb a tree but, as you look at it from your current position, there's no sturdy place as foothold. You might become discouraged and frustrated, since you want those fruits on the top but as you take a couple of steps *around* the tree, there it is, a gnarl that you can use, that you couldn't notice from the first position. From this new perspective, now you have *more options* opening up for you. Frustration and discouragement are gone. New behaviors are available.

Similarly, when you look at *selling* from new perspectives – for instance, like the one I suggest - you'll find yourself more resourceful, confident and comfortable talking with people about the product or service you're promoting and asking for what you want in return for it. You'll act *congruently*, as your inner understandings become aligned now with your outer actions.

Three Parts

In Part 1 I'll uncover the current view that people have about *selling* and *salespersons*. In a highly "politically incorrect" manner, I will be blunt about why we arrived to this situation and why most salespersons are stressed out and frustrated, making *selling* a profession with such a high turnover rate.

In Part 2 I'll bring to your attention the original meaning of the concept of *selling* - as it was used thousands of years ago. I will explore it in order to extract principles and guidelines for the proposed "Heart to Heart (H2H)" model of selling.

In Part 3 you'll find what refinements you can do inside yourself, what shifts in *attitudes* and *understandings* you can make, so that selling will become enjoyable and fun for you. "Heart to Heart Selling" is not a collection of new techniques *to do*, but it's something you **become**. To facilitate that, I elaborate a bit on a few concepts that I consider essential for you to really grasp on the model that I propose. These concepts are not new and I noticed that people have various opinions about what they mean – that's why I wanted to bring all of us to a common base, a mutual understanding that would be helpful. Look at those chapters as the letters of the alphabet: they may seem abstract at the first glance, but when you put them together and "arrange them in words", they will make perfect sense and will help glue everything in one solid and natural *way of being.*

Time to time, when I'll make a point, I'll also play the "devil's advocate" to proactively answer the readers who might raise counter-arguments against the idea that I am building. You'll see paragraphs titled "Yes, but..."; I am anticipating those counter-arguments and I am answering them the way I would if those persons were in front of me.

I also included paragraphs titled "Think of this for a moment..." They will provide you with a metaphor, an example of sorts, to help you recognize the validity of the principle I am building, by showing you how it applies to other common aspects of life.

Through the book you'll see paragraphs titled "Experience/ Exercise". These are exercises designed to give you a *direct experience* of what I am talking about. I encourage you to *playfully engage* with them fully, without reservation. Some of them I designed myself, others I borrowed from the trainings I attended in the past. I have personally done all of them. I know they will achieve their purpose when done wholeheartedly.

An Intellectual understanding is important, but without an *experience* at the sensorial level, there are little chances for *transformation* to occur. I'll remind you, true "Heart to Heart Salesmanship" is not something that you "do", but it's something you "become".

PART 1:

CURRENT PARADIGM OF SELLING

CHAPTER 4:

What Is Selling, According to the Contemporary Paradigm?

"Words are not the things we are speaking about."
Alfred Korzybski

I wanted to understand what "selling" is, so I searched in the dictionary. This is what I found:

- "to persuade or induce someone to buy (something)" - Dictionary.com

- "The last step in the chain of commerce where a buyer exchanges cash for a seller's good or service" - www.businessdictionary.com

- "to give something to someone else in return for money" - Cambridge dictionary

Think of this for a moment...

The phone rings. An overly enthusiastic voice is telling me that I am "their most valued customer" and continues with an obviously scripted eulogy for their new service that they can activate for me right now! They never asked me if I have time to listen to their offer; they never bothered to inquire about my needs or wants; but they were ready to take my payment information.

Can you relate to this?

Last week I stopped at the dealership for an oil change. While waiting, I walked around through the parking lot, looking at the new cars. Out of nowhere, a salesman popped-up, showing me his formal "smiling face #5", smiling only with his teeth, his eyes remaining focused and cold. He started to recite his canned *opening questions*, with an attitude of "you're mine!", while striving to disguise his hope that I would buy a car today.

Since I am a salesman, too, I politely explained that I thank him for his effort, but I am not interested in his offer. What do I notice? He starts proving to me that he really incorporated the slogan "don't take *no* for an answer". Perhaps it was his sales manager who imposed this, perhaps he read it in a book or he heard it on some motivational speech. Whatever the case, look! Now he pressures me with childish "leading questions", like "you want to save money, don't you?" or "what kind of features you'd like your car to have?" (I never said I wanted a car, to start with!)

I began to feel a bit uncomfortable and uneasy. It's an interestingly awkward feeling, when you are pressured to give only certain answers, because to answer differently would mean that you're not entirely sane! You feel manipulated into stating some things, which are logical, but when connected with the current context, they push you into accepting to act in a particular way: since you value saving money, and this particular deal is good only for today, then this means you should buy now! They pressure you to do it, implying that by not taking advantage of this opportunity you will feel guilty and ashamed of yourself for the rest of your life.

It's a broken logic, some sort of double bind and it's not feeling good. I call this "manipulation", in a bad way.

If you've ever been in a similar position, you know that feeling, don't you? If you're like most people, you're probably - at least - annoyed by these kinds of situations. You had no 'connection' with that salesperson and you didn't feel like wanting to have anything to do with them in the future. Simply put – you didn't like them.

You know it's true. It's "a fact". People don't like salespersons. Consequently, because you inherently want to "be liked", **you** don't want to be associated with that title.

You don't want to be called or seen as a "salesperson."

Look in the Dictionary

And yet - according to the current understanding of "what selling is" - that salesperson was behaving "normally", as they "should.

How come? Well, considering the definition we found in the dictionary, *selling* is intimately connected with the result of the process. That is, selling means "getting the result, the outcome" - otherwise the process was Not *selling*, the salesperson did Not *sell*... The dictionary says that 'to sell' means *to get them to buy, to exchange cash*, implying that they give you their money. In this light, those people can rightfully consider that they are actually selling properly. If selling is about persuasion and convincing and doing whatever it takes in order to obtain the outcome, then this is it: they bring arguments and use tactics in order to convince people to buy.

Yes, but...

You may say: "Yes, but this is what selling means, look in the dictionary!"

Good point. Let's look at how a dictionary is made, to start with.

The purpose of a dictionary is to show how people are actually *using* those words, currently – not to tell them what to think and how to use those words. When somebody writes a dictionary, they simply study *the language as it is used*, they study the *current usage* of the words. They might take all the books or articles that have been written and analyze how a particular word has been utilized, with what meanings and in what contexts.

To say that "this is what selling means, because it is written in the dictionary" is a sophism, a false logic, because the description we read in the dictionary was taken from how people are currently defining it, in the first place. The definition from the dictionary is merely *a reflection* of the meaning that people assign to the word, as they use it.

That means that a dictionary is not "the truth" which is "set in stone". It only shows the general cultural perspective, the common paradigm, the ongoing usage of that word.

Moreover, we all alter the meaning of the words, as we speak.

"The editors who write dictionaries simply try to keep up with us, as we change the language. They are watching what we say. [...] They try to describe what we do.", tells us the language historian Anne Curzan, in her TED talk. "[they] can give you a sense of the range of opinions about contested usage. [they] listen to what other people are saying and writing, [they] look at usage, at how we use it."

Does that imply that all of us decide what words mean? "Yes, it does!" she concludes, "and it always has. [...] There is no objective dictionary authority as the final arbiter about what words mean."

New words appear all the time. "Consider *google* as a verb or *invite* as a noun." She also brings up the fact that "words are changing meaning" and that "semantic shifts are common".

She gives the example of the word "peruse", to which the American Heritage Dictionary attached an *Usage Note: "Peruse has long meant 'to read thoroughly'... But the word is often used more loosely, to mean simply 'to read'... Further extension of the word to mean 'to glance over, skim' has traditionally been considered an error, but our ballot results suggest that it is becoming somewhat more acceptable. When asked about the sentence 'I only had a moment to peruse the manual quickly', 66% of the Usage Panel found it unacceptable in 1988, 58% in 1999, and 48% in 2011."*

Here there are some other examples that she brings to our attention:

- The word "nice" used to mean "silly";
- The word "decimate" used to mean "to kill one in every ten".

Dictionaries are an useful resource, but they don't have the authority to *impose* on us what a word means – they only show how that word is used *today*. The meaning of words changes over time, according to the current explanation of the experience that people have about that concept.

So, if I Define What a Word Means...

Knowing all this, I started to wonder **if** and **how** the concept of *selling* suffered any *meaning shift* over time, in people's understanding of it. In other words, I will not simply "make up" an arbitrary meaning for *selling*, just to fit my "agenda". I will show you the *original meaning* of the word "sell", as it was used thousands of years ago. And, if you'll find that the suggested meaning will serve you better in your selling career, you are free to adopt it.

To be clear, I am not implying that you "should" repudiate the current meaning of the concept of selling or that you "should" revert to the old meaning. No. I am only demonstrating that you have the liberty to "tweak" the meaning of a particular concept, if the "popular" meaning does not serve you.

Think of this for a moment...

We are doing this, anyhow, in regards with all sorts of concepts in our lives. We choose the *meaning* of what a particular concept, according to our liking, to serve our purpose.

From a scientific viewpoint, *smoking* means inhaling nicotine, formaldehyde, ammonia, hydrogen cyanide, and so forth. However, for most smokers, it's only "smoke", which changes the entire meaning of it and allows them to use cigarettes without much thought.

Driving, for some people, it's a pleasure. For others, though, it means a total hassle.

People use the **same** word, but describe and evoke an entirely different experience, because they hold a different understanding of what that concept means to them.

Some people told me that changing the current paradigm where selling is associated with deceiving it's an impossible task. My answer is this: From antiquity until the late 1800's, the idea of "going to the doctor" was associated with the procedure of bloodletting. However, nowadays we cannot even conceive that. And all started from the doctors engaging differently with their procedures! When salespersons will start engaging differently with the manner they sell, eventually the cultural associations will change, as well, and a new reality will emerge.

Now we know that words and concepts suffer a meaning shift. Let's see how people currently perceive the concept of *selling* and how did we arrive in this situation?

CHAPTER 5:

How Do People Feel about Selling and Salespeople and, Most Importantly, Why Is It So?

"If a problem can be solved at all, to understand it and to know what to do about it are the same thing."
Alan Watts

Think of this for a moment...

A nice lady that I interviewed told me about her experience: "It was Saturday, about 7pm, when I heard somebody knocking on my door. I wasn't expecting anybody and, since I am 60 years old, my first reaction was to ignore it. However, the knocking continued – perhaps they saw the lights on. My son was with me, so I decided to open the door.

There was this young girl who introduced herself as the representative of a cable TV company, other than the one I was using. I told her that I am OK with what I have, but she stated that she could save me $600 per year. Now, that was weird, I thought, since I didn't tell her what my current charges were. Moreover, she started to slander my current provider and to brag how much better *they* are. I wanted her to stop and to leave me alone. "I'm sorry, it's late and I need to go now", I said but she wouldn't let me close the door – she *literally* put her foot on my door! I had to call my son, who came and resolved a situation which could have degenerate into something ugly."

Remember for a moment the examples from the beginning of the previous chapter. How do you feel when a telemarketer interrupts you and then starts reading a scripts pressuring you to buy something? What's your first gut reaction when you go to a car dealership and the salesperson immediately jumps at you, pushing you to buy a car, just because "they have a great deal, today only"?

If you say that you are enjoying those interactions and you are looking forward to have more of them, you're either new or special. Either way, it's not the norm. Most people are annoyed by a salesperson who hustles them and – without having been invited to do so - starts telling them all the reasons why they should buy their product, and buy it now!

Let's step back for a moment and notice what lies behind this type of interaction, underneath the "politically correct" verbal dressing. When the salesperson starts to convince, persuade, manipulate – and generally, pressure - the client to buy, the salesperson's aim is to '*take* something *from* the client', to 'make them buy'. The selling process is made 'about the salesperson' and their advantage. The client's role is to 'be a victim'.

This kind of behavior, adopted over time by many salespersons (not all of them, for sure!), gave rise in our society to a general bias against salespeople.

"When you push on people, they often push back", noticed James Tripp, transformative coach, author of the Hypnosis Without Trance concept.

"Yes, but..."

During the conversations that I had with other salespersons, some of them grew offended by the ideas I stated above and defied them. They went to the extreme of affirming that *everybody loves salespeople.*

If you think that, ask 10 of your friends what's their gut reaction when they pick up the phone and an overly-enthusiastic voice tells them "congratulations", that they are a "valued customer", they just won a drawing they never entered and all they need to do is to buy "this product, today only". I'm curious, how many of them will say that they would love to receive more of those phone calls.

Thus, the prospects reject the salespersons, the salespersons feel bad about it, and that's how this "invisible war" appeared between them. This kind of "bad selling" became so frequent, that now people automatically think of it when they meet a salesperson. It became a *cultural meme*, an implicit association: all salespersons practice "bad selling".

However, the main distinction is that:

People resent the salesperson only because of the cultural association with bad selling.

In other words:

People don't inherently resent the salesperson, but the bad selling.

The question that rose in my mind was: Are salespersons

inherently "bad people"?

I certainly don't think so.

What is it that makes the salespersons behave in this manner? What is it that pressures *them* to act so selfishly?

CHAPTER 6:

How Are the Salespersons Trained to Think?

"Seek first to understand, then to be understood."
Stephen R. Covey, The Seven Habits of Highly Effective People

It's 7 am and I am in the middle of the weekly sales meeting, with my sales manager and with my colleagues. The sales manager is talking. He was recently promoted because of his good results as a salesman. Now he trains his team how to think and what to do. As he said, he wants us to become "clones" of his, so that we will be as successful as he is.

Every sales meeting is filled with motivational urges for action, like "the client doesn't know how greatly he could benefit from my product until you convince him"; or, "If I took *no* for an answer without pushing for a *yes* I wouldn't have made half of my sales"; or, "When two people meet, one of them is buying: will it be you or the customer?" (have you heard that one?...)

Although those statements sound true and valid, they make me uncomfortable, for some reason. I tried to open a conversation with my sales manager, but I shortly realized that his philosophy of life is "he who doesn't entirely agree with what I say, is against me". Any conversation that would imply that he is less than 100% right was forcefully dismissed.

The Salesperson Knows Better...

I stepped back and I looked at those statements, trying to get a sense of the source of my discomfort about them. I realized that, for any of those affirmations to be true, the implied presupposition behind them is that the process of selling is "about making a sale" and it's only "about the benefit of the salesperson", ignoring the client's *consciousness*. The client is regarded – more or less – as an object, whose permission is not necessary to make changes upon it. If the salesperson believes that their product is "good" for the client, then the salesperson is entitled to do whatever they consider necessary to "make" the client buy.

Just like when we change the oil on our car's engine: we know it's good for the engine, so we do it. No need to ask the engine's permission. That would be silly, wouldn't it?

However, people are not cars. While a car has no say in the oil-changing operation, a human being it's an organic process. Although all sales trainings "talk" about the importance of "creating relationships", they quickly shift their focus on techniques and strategies to "make people buy". Nobody seems to notice that this attitude is not at all conducive to *nurturing relationships.*

Think of this for a moment...

How open are you to enter a relationship with someone who obviously wants something *from* you?

You've been a child, at one moment of your life. When your parents "forced" you to do something, "making" you behave in a certain way, how did you feel in *that* moment? Perhaps *now* you see that it was a good and valuable lesson for you – but in *that* moment, did you feel understood and respected, as a human being?

If you had a choice, would you have "bought" from them?

As a child, my father obligated me to eat soup, because "it was good for me". Looking back, I realize that he did a good thing, but in those moments I felt resentment and frustration. I felt imposed upon, not understood and disrespected. Obviously, at the time, there wasn't much I could do about it.

But, when someone tries to do that to me now, I choose to "not buy" their idea.

Why?

First of all, if I were to change my life by adopting someone else's ideas, I would want to have a sense that they have my wellness at heart. I don't get that when they care more about the rightfulness of their idea than they care about me.

Second, I don't think that an idea or a thing is "good" in and of itself, separated from my own experience of it. When someone imposes their "good" idea on me, my experience of it will be less than pleasant, so I'll never make "good use" of it.

When you treat your clients as if they are children who need to "be told" what to do and who can be "imposed" on, how can you expect them to feel understood, respected and wanting to have more interaction with you?

The only reason people buy things is to improve the situation they currently experience. That means *they* need to recognize *value* in that thing. If *they* find no value in it – even if hundreds of other people did – you have no business continuing selling it to them. Why? Because your product will be valuable to them only to the extent that they will use it properly - which they won't if they don't value it enough or if they have a highly unpleasant experience linked to it.

If you start pressuring, convincing, persuading and even manipulating the client that they *should* recognize the value where it's not [i.e., for them], this has big chances to turn the interaction into something unpleasant.

This is exactly the part which makes most salespersons feel awkward about their selling profession – because they think that *this* is what they are supposed to do.

Also, this is exactly what created the cultural stereotype about *selling.*

The Carrot and the Stick for a Salesperson

One big cause for this attitude is the manner in which sales managers and salespeople are compensated for their work. Indeed, they make money only when the customer buys. Thus, I cannot blame them for focusing on "making the sale" (however, see Chapter 15 "What is, really, the purpose of Selling in business?").

Of course, they know about "creating relationships" part and they talk about it, but their focus remains on "making the sale", obviously. They are pressured with "sales meetings" about "sales plans" and "sales reports".

So, what do salespeople do? Since they know that on the next sales meeting the manager will heavily scold them if their "numbers" don't look good, they go out with a single focus on their minds: to *make a sale,* to *make somebody buy their product.* The "creating relationships" part becomes secondary. So, they importune people, pressure them to buy a product which brings no value to their lives and annoy them with their insistence. Also, because of the pressure that's set upon them by their sales managers (and, generally, by the company's policy), they will tend to employ manipulation, persuasion and deceiving as tools to force the transaction to go through.

Salespersons are trained in the sense that, in order for them to have done a good job selling, the clients would *have* to buy. This understanding makes them **attached** to the outcome, and **needy**. And, as Steve Chandler and Rich Litvin put it in their book, The Prosperous Coach, "neediness is creepy". Or, as Jamie Smart says: "Needy is like <client repellant>!"

This attitude is exactly what created the problem, in the first place.

What problem?

The problem of a bad reputation for the profession of Selling.

A Meme Was Created - Let's Make Another One

Can you foresee how this behavior is prone to bring a bad name to the company itself or even generalized to the entire industry? If I mention "used car salesman" – does this line sound familiar?

The purpose of the previous chapter was to show that salespersons are pressured to behave this way, by the business model of the company they work for. The good news is that if they were really encouraged to focus on facilitating the emergence of relationships and serving those prospects, soon they will not need to worry about *prospecting* or *convincing* people to buy, because the happy people they served are becoming clients who buy again and again, and bring their friends, too.

Every successful salesperson that I interviewed does this.

All you can do (as a salesperson) is to suitably *facilitate* for the clients *to feel for themselves* the *value* in your offer. Please note that I didn't say that you "build" the value – a concept that's much used in the selling industry, although entirely inappropriate. When the client finds – on their own terms - *value* in something, it's like them 'falling in love' with it. You cannot "build" love; you can only encourage love to grow, by seeding the right conditions. I'll show you how that works, as you read through.

Many salespersons have a sense that the current model of selling causes them to fell inadequate. They feel an incongruence, a mismatch between their inner values and the outer behavior that they are taught to do, as selling. This internal conflict causes them to produce certain subtle gestures, voice tonalities or words choices that the client notices - although not [always] at the conscious level. The client realizes that the salesperson is hiding something, that he is not entirely honest about something. As a result, the client's trust in the salesperson starts to deteriorate and they will choose to not buy.

The salespersons became aware of this dynamic and they try hard to alleviate this internal conflict which caused this problem. The sales trainers also became aware about the gravity of this phenomenon and they started to teach ways to mitigate it. Let's see what are the common strategies for that.

CHAPTER 7:

What Are the Salespersons Currently Doing to Overcome this Issue?

"If the ladder is not leaning against the right wall, every step we take just gets us to the wrong place faster."
Stephen R. Covey, The 7 Habits of Highly Effective People

Most problems that people experience have their roots on the *worldview* that people hold: the *concepts*, the *beliefs* they have about the world, the *perspectives* they choose when looking at the world around them.

One way to deal with that is to **replace the concept**: "I am not a *salesperson*, I am a *consultant*". Some salespeople try to disguise what they really do by calling themselves "account manager", "product consultant" or "technical representative".

This can work for some people, if they truly adopt the *meanings* of the new concept.

Many salespersons - particularly in the fields of therapy, coaching, and such – reframe their selling, calling it **serving,** instead. "I'm not *selling*, I am *serving*", they say, in order to distance themselves from the "salesperson" title.

Why would they do that? Well, exactly because of the current paradigm of the concept of selling. They know that the moment people label them as a "salesperson", people will also assign to them all the other negative implications (pushy, arrogant, insensitive, etc) – although they did not exhibit any of those disagreeable traits.

There is a problem with this solution, of simply changing the name of the activity: no matter what titles they invent to 'disguise' what they do, deep inside they know that they are 'a salesperson'. This is what's written on their job description: "salesperson", not "server" or "relationship creator". As long as, for them, the meaning of one is different than the meaning of the other, they will know that they are not true to themselves – and this will only induce an additional tension and incongruence in their system.

Others try to grow in themselves the belief that "it's the client that's wrong". Perhaps you heard this: "if the client doesn't realize how many benefits they can get if they buy my product, then it's their loss". However, this is not really a 'solution', but rather a way to discharge the negative frustration.

If the above strategies don't work, another way to deal with this is to **change your understanding** *about what the concept* **means** *to you:* if selling means to you that you "need to *convince* somebody to *buy*" and if you find this dis-empowering, then you may define a new meaning for *selling*. You may need to re-write it from inside-out. This is what I am proposing to you in this book.

Any of the above *could* work for you. But if you continue the practice of talking without listening, of deceiving and manipulating the customer into "taking action", of 'being pushy', cornering the prospect and 'not taking *no* for an answer', of making the sale "about you and your commission" instead of making it "about the customer and solving their problem" – you are missing the point.

It's not about the salesperson, but rather about the way they sell.

And the way people sell is *always* in coherence with their *understanding* of what *selling* means.

At this point, I think it's necessary that I make this clarification: by no means do I imply that salespersons are "bad people". I don't even think that "bad people" exist. There may be some people who choose to behave in a certain manner because they *think* they are doing a good thing, where, in fact, they are causing other people to suffer. Similarly, if some salespersons behave in the way I described, it's only because of their understanding about what selling means. They do what they do because they *believe* that they are supposed to, that this is how it should be and this is what selling means.

Actually, most salespeople became more and more aware of the inner conflict I mentioned at the end of Chapter 6. That's exactly the reason why they do their best to redefine and reframe what they do (see Chapter 7). These are signs that the current model of selling is not effective anymore and that a new model is required.

But this paradigm change proves to be a slow process. What keeps in place this old model of selling? Why is this process of change so slow?

CHAPTER 8:

What Keeps in Place this Old Model of Selling?

"You cannot control what happens to you, but you can control your attitude toward what happens to you, and in that, you will be mastering change rather than allowing it to master you."
Brian Tracy

Once a person adopts a particular perspective, it becomes a part of "who they are". Because they adopt that belief at the identity level, it solidifies. It's like the Ouroboros motif symbolizing the serpent eating its own tail and suggesting something that keeps re-creating itself: the person believes that this is who they are; and because this is who they are, it just seems natural to hold the belief that they *are* that way!

In my experience, a first and important step in helping people to change a disempowering belief is for them to become aware that whatever they think they "are" it's only an idea, a belief, a thought which cannot be "the truth". In other words, it's not that they "are" in a particular way, but rather they are "doing" some behaviors (for example, it's not that they "are" smokers, but they "do" smoking).

Secondly, I help them witness the psychological processes that they use to re-create those behaviors. Those processes are so subtle and so easy to activate, that they arrive to think that this is "how it should be" – but once they become aware of their existence and activity, people gain the capacity to alter them.

A similar process happens at the level of a community. The sum beliefs held by a community is called 'culture'. As a community adopts a belief, a perspective, that belief becomes part of that culture. People in that community end up identifying themselves with that belief. Then, some psychological and sociological processes come at play and keep that belief in place.

It's called 'cultural inertia' or 'social inertia' and represents the tendency to resist change. But this is just an impersonal term which camouflages the fact that it's *us* – the actual members of the community - that perpetuate that cultural belief, by perpetuating it within ourselves.

In Chapter 4 I wanted to show you that we "do" the current meaning of the concept of *selling* and it's false to believe that this meaning is something which "is" independent of our own doing. I showed you that it is *us* that define what a word means and that the dictionary simply reflects our current understanding of it (i.e., instead of believing that the dictionary definition is "written in stone" and that we should conform to it without questioning it, just because it's there).

Now let's take a look at some of the psychological and sociological processes that people do to perpetuate the current perspective over the concept of *selling*. This is not a comprehensive list and I don't even aim for that. I only want to make you aware that we all contribute to re-creating the current paradigm of **selling** and that *we* have the power to change it if it doesn't help us anymore.

Classical Conditioning

Although not all salespersons experience that, perhaps most of you can relate to *procrastinating* before making sales calls or to feeling awkward when asking for money, at the end of the presentation. Why does that happen?

First and foremost, please understand that there's nothing "wrong with you". It's a natural phenomenon at work.

There are many models to explain how this state of things developed, but the simplest way to do it is, perhaps, through *classical conditioning* theory.

Think of this for a moment...

Couple of years ago I had a fantastic vacation, in an exotic place, together with a wonderful person. We really had a great time, enjoying everything and finding fun in all experiences. All the while, we were continually hearing a particular song, which was broadcasted a lot, for some reason.

Coming back home, I engaged back in my work, learning, writing, working on my business. That vacation became a nice memory, somewhere on the back of my mind, almost forgotten. Then, one day, I hear at the radio that song that was always present in my hearing during that forgotten vacation. All of a sudden, a flush of emotions surfaced out of nowhere, instantly carrying me back to that time and place. I "was there", feeling the feelings I had all that time, seeing those fascinating places, experiencing all that fun and enjoyment.

Most probably you heard about *classical conditioning* and about

Pavlov's experiment with the dog; I will briefly and simplistically describe it for those who didn't:

- He shows the dog the food (let's call this "real stimulus", although scientifically it's called differently);

- At the sight of the food, the dog unconsciously starts to salivate, as a natural response (let's call this "real response");

- *Simultaneously* with showing the food, Pavlov rings a bell (we'll name this "conditioned stimulus").

He noticed that, after a few repetitions of this scenario, he could ring the bell without showing any food, and the dog would still unconsciously salivate.

In other words, although initially only the sight of the food (the "real stimulus") created the salivation (the "real response"), now, after a few runs, the salivation is produced by the ring of the bell alone (the "conditioned stimulus"). It's said that the dog "associated" the "conditioned stimulus" with the "real stimulus" and it is believed that now, at the sound of the bell, the dog's "mind" *expects with certainty* that the food will appear, so it reacts accordingly, bringing up the unconscious (real) response.

How does this relate to the selling situations?

Consider this: every time you are involved in a sales situation ("real stimulus"), you feel uneasy and uncomfortable ("real response") – either because someone pressures you to buy or because you are selling something and the client treats you with disrespect. Obviously, during this time, at some level, you are *thinking* <This is a sales situation.> ("the conditioned stimulus") After a while, you develop an unconscious association between "sales situations" and "feeling uncomfortable". The stronger the feeling that you experience in that situation, the quicker and more powerful the association. Then, only the *thought* about "sales situations" makes you "feel uncomfortable".

Just as – in my initial story – the feelings of enjoyment became associated with the song that was played on the radio, in the same way your feelings of "un-easy-ness" became associated with the idea of "sales situations". When the idea of *selling* comes to your awareness, the *discomfort* is instantly following.

Yes, but...

I heard people saying: "But I am a rational human being. I know that selling is necessary for developing my business. I should be strong and do it anyway".

The way our minds work is rather intricate. Without going deeply into its dynamics, I will only say that it is our *unconscious mind* that rules the way we live our lives. Also, it doesn't respond to the *conscious* reasoning, willpower or arguments, but only to the *representations* that we built about a particular aspect of our lives (in particular *feelings* and *internal pictures*). For instance, if you associated *fear* to *public speaking*, you may try to "force" yourself to stand up and talk, using your willpower, but you know already how that will go.

Experience/ Exercise

Right now, using all the *willpower* you can activate, whatever you do, whatever happens... don't think of a **red cat**, having big **red** soft eyes, sitting in a little **red** tree, looking at you and going "meeeooowww"!

Oopps, what's happening? Unless you're semantically trained, most probably you were thinking of a **red cat**, now!

Simply by holding this association, and especially because it sits at the unconscious level, you are perpetuating in your community the association "selling equals discomfort". It's just like a seed, that you planted in the ground, and it grows all by itself.

An easy way to dissolve this association is to 'be mindful' about it, to recognize its existence and to become aware of its work in the moment. Notice how you start to feel uncomfortable, awkward or shy when you enter or think about a sales situation. That's because you are watching the world 'Through' those feelings and, as a result, you end up believing that those feelings are telling you something about the situation you're facing. Instead, realize that you have this experience only because you are thinking some thoughts, 'about' that situation – you are simply feeling your thinking. Moreover, realize that, whatever feelings you are feeling, those feelings cannot tell you anything about the future. The "purpose" of our feelings is merely to tell us about the kind of thinking we do. So, look 'At' those feelings, observe them without trying to hide them or push them away and – more importantly - without taking them as "messengers" of what's going to happen. See them for what they are: the "flip side" of your thoughts, that come and go. Realize that you don't have to take those feelings into consideration when you go about doing something.

Labeling

Labeling is the social phenomenon through which – simply put – one ends up thinking, feeling and behaving according to the social label with which one has been labeled.

When you are "in sales" – promoting your own product or working for another company – the society applies this label to you: you *are* a 'salesperson'. Once you have this label, you implicitly carry and perpetuate all of the stereotypes that culture has about the concept of selling, whatever they are at a particular moment in time. Since people's expectations are for you to think and behave in a certain manner, you'll experience a strong tendency to actualize it.

The *self* is socially constructed and continuously redefined according to the interactions with the people in your community – not always, but in the vast majority of cases. Thus, you construct your self-image using the feedback of how others respond to you and from *how you think they are thinking* about you. The way you have been "tagged" may pressure you to adopt the tag's behavioral implications, as part of your identity.

Some people are ok with that, and, unfortunately, they actually *become* that salesperson that's portrayed in movies like "Glengarry Glen Ross" or "The Wolf of Wall Street".

Others, though, have different values and don't want to become that type of person. However, the pressure coming from labeling often induces a "silent internal conflict", conducive to passivity, procrastination and even depression. Not a happy feeling.

To counter the pressure of complying with these cultural expectations, you need to build for yourself a stronger sense of the reality *you* want to create for yourself. This requires that you are clear about what is it that you want to create and to make sure that it aligns with your personal values. Then go on creating that.

Fear of Rejection

Most sales trainings ridicule the "fear of rejection" that salespersons often experience, but I find this practice as counter-productive and ineffective. As human beings, we are social creatures and it is essential for us to experience social interaction. We need acceptance from others. We have a basic need for love and belongingness. Our own survival depends on it – although much less today than thousands of years ago, when people who were excluded from the tribe would most probably die, alone in the wilderness.

Thus, *rejection* is a serious threat, as a concern over social exclusion. People with high rejection sensitivity have troubles expressing opinions, making requests of others, they are easily hurt by negative feedback from others and they even tend to anxiously *expect* social rejection. Then, in order to avoid this threat (i.e., of being rejected) they end up avoiding the situations in which such rejection might arise. They will over-do things that they know are "safe" from this perspective. I can recognize myself in many of these descriptions; "been there, done that", as they say.

By holding this fear, we are projecting it all around us and we end up creating and perpetuating a reality which confirms that fear.

However, this "fear of rejection" can become overwhelming

only **If you expect to be accepted by** *everybody.*

It is this *generalization* that creates the anxiety, this *need for everybody to say yes to you* – and it is, indeed, absurd to expect that *everybody* will like and accept you. Nobody has that. A particular person may be liked by *more* people than you are, but still, there will be plenty of people who would not like them.

Some people will love you, whatever you do. Others will build a wall between you and them and turn their back on you, whatever you do. Moreover, most of the 7 billion people on this planet will not even know that you exist.

Consider the people living thousands of years ago: they didn't need to be accepted by ALL tribes in the world, but only by the one that they would trust to protect them. In those times, this was a 'survival necessity'. Today we may 'want' to be accepted by a particular social group, but that's not anymore a 'survival necessity'. As a species, we tremendously increased our flexibility in creating opportunities to thrive and hugely reduced the survival threats.

The more accepted you feel in your intimate social community, as a 'support system' (that is, the more you are able to make friends and get along with them), the more you'll feel good in your own skin and the more able you will become to deal with situations where *some* of the people might not take in your ideas. Your "fear of rejection" will diminish on its own and you'll start creating a different kind of reality around you.

This is also a good moment to remember that your feelings are simply telling you about the quality of your thinking, and they have no way of predicting how other people will respond to you.

(on a side note, one thing that you may have already realized is that people are generally open to new friendships, when they feel safe, secure and appreciated for what they are, not for what you hope to *take from* them)

Another useful distinction is to avoid taking that refusal personally, at the identity level. Logically, you probably know that when the prospect says 'no', they refuse *your offer* and that there is no reason for you to feel "less than..." This tendency to take the refusals *personally* comes (as some people revealed) from a deep, unconscious belief that you "should" be able to "make them buy", if you were a "good salesperson".

But, is this really how the things are?

Think of this for a moment...

Suppose you and I meet and I am offering you $10 if you accept to put mud on your face. Most probably you'll say "no". Does that really have to mean that I AM a "poor salesperson"?

Or,

Suppose I am now offering you to buy a pink elephant. Also suppose you have no use of such thing (because you live in downtown New York) and you refuse it. Is there any reason for me to feel that I "should" be able to "make you" buy it? Is there any reason for me to feel "incomplete", "incompetent" or "a poor salesperson"?

It may be an interesting conversation to have with someone who would argue that I should...

Think of this for a moment...

By the way, what happens when you **replace "rejection" with "non-acceptance"**?

As in: It's not that "they rejected my offer", but rather "they didn't accept my offer"...

Experience/ Exercise

An effective 'game' to play in order to stop taking refusals personally is the 'No' Game. Adopt the most natural and detached attitude and go beyond your comfort zone: ask a stranger for something and accept their "no" with total ease. Then do it again – until you get used to hearing the word "no" and having the experience that, actually, no catastrophe is happening to you. Celebrate your "no's".

I believe it was Jamie Smart who experimented with going to a McDonald's and – with a straight face, as it was the most natural thing to do – he asked for a large pizza with pinnacle and mushrooms. When he was told that they don't sell those, he said "Oh, really? OK, then, what do you have?" – just as if he never heard of McDonald's in his entire life and he made an honest mistake.

I know of somebody who is going to strangers to the mall, asking them for $100. If someone asks, he tells them that the money is for a charity (which is true, by the way). He gets many "no's", but you'll be surprised to find out that he also gets "yes's".

Personally, I asked people in grocery stores if I can have their cart, because I forgot to bring one from the entrance. Obviously, they refused. I thanked them and I left, as if nothing had happened.

Remember, the purpose of this exercise is to get used to hearing the word "no" and have an experience that it's harmless. Moreover, you'll get used to actually ASK for what you want, without allowing your feelings to interfere and without the *need* of receiving only "yes's".

Your Understanding of What Selling Means

Perhaps you believe that *selling* is about *you* and what *you* want, and that it means that you *have to convince* the client *to buy* – see Chapter 6 "How are the Salespersons trained to think?"

Experience/ Exercise

Choose a partner to talk to for a few minutes – either in person or by phone. This is a two-part exercise. On each part you'll choose a different attitude, a different focus, while carrying the conversation. The subject of the conversation is irrelevant. What matters is your *attitude* and your *focus* during that conversation. Pay attention to how you feel in each of the situations. Then ask your partner to tell you what was their experience, in each of those cases.

In the first part, your focus should be on *getting* them to *like you*, to *approve of you*, to *accept you* as a friend. In other words, focus on *getting under their skin*. Moreover, direct your focus on how to *make them* give you some money. However, all the time, do your best to hide your intentions under a mask of "being friendly".

For the second part of the exercise, do this:

- First, to de-potentiate the previous state, shake your body a bit, look around and, if it's possible to do it safely, spin a couple of times, forwards and backwards. Pay attention to your breathing for a few seconds. Feel your legs. Slow down and listen to the sounds around you. Defocus your eyes and expand your vision into the peripheral.

- Remember a friend of yours with whom you feel mostly connected with. Remember a specific situation, where you were together, feeling good in their presence, feeling good about yourself and having a sense of deep connection with them. Notice that you do not want anything *from* them, but you have all the goodwill to do something *for* them, to make them a *gift,* if – and only if - they would choose to accept it.

- As you feel that, gently turn your attention towards your partner for this exercise, with the attitude of allowing that good feeling of deep, genuine and candid connection to emerge all by itself between you two. Know that the connection already exists, and all you need to do is to *allow* it to arise in your awareness – *there's nothing you need to deliberately do.* When talking to them, gently put aside any ulterior motive that your mind wants to bring up. Listen to them empathically, for the sheer experience of understanding them. There's no need to think at what you should say next. Just *be there* with them, resonating with them and allowing yourself to get a sense of who they really are and what they feel. Be the first person in their lives who listens to them so attentively and empathically, simply willing to learn about them without any judgment.

- As you do that, if – and only if – you notice a way that you could help them, gently ask *permission* to tell them about a possible solution you might have. Let go of any need for them to accept it. Maintain your serenity, your equanimity in regards to their response. You know that a gift that is forced ceases to be useful.

What differences did you notice in your interaction with your partner, in those two different situations? Which one was more pleasant and led to a good feeling, where both of you wanted to have more of such interactions? Ask *them,* in which case they felt a stronger connection with you and wanting to continue the interaction with you?

Think of this for a moment...

What's your *primary focus* and your *attitude* when you enter a sales interaction with a potential client?

Most salespersons involuntarily adopt the first type of attitude, simply because that's what they were taught that selling is about! In doing so, they spread and nurture in their community the belief that selling is disingenuous, insincere and uncomfortable.

However, if they were to adopt the type of interaction described on the second part of the exercise above, they will feel better about themselves and the people they interact with will feel at ease, trusting, appreciated and taken care of.

Wouldn't be nice if people will end up associating these kinds of feelings with the concept of selling?

I realize that it is only human to take the path of least resistance and behave according to the current cultural memes – it's easier to eat the cake or to smoke the cigarette, than to resist it. However, the "trick" is not to 'resist', but to decide and commit to find joy and satisfaction in making a different choice.

Why would you do that, though?

In doing my research for this book, I interviewed many salespeople. I noticed that the most successful ones (not only financially, but also from a happiness standpoint) hold a different perspective about selling than the salespeople who struggle financially or who are deeply dissatisfied about themselves (although financially ok). They choose to entertain only the thoughts they consider useful in *creating* the kind of *reality* they want for themselves. They accept that some people will choose to not accept their offer, simply because they don't see value in it or perhaps it's not the right time for them. They let go of the need that everybody should accept them. They give priority to *connecting* with their client, instead of "winning them over". They want to do business only with "people who believe what they believe."

CHAPTER 9:

Successful Salespeople – How Do They Understand Selling...

"Always recognize that human individuals are ends, and do not use them as means to your end."
Immanuel Kant

I want to reinforce a note in regards to the things I wrote so far.

By no stretch do I imply that *every* single person believes that selling is a disease or that *every* salesperson on earth is a deceiver.

Not at all.

As a matter of fact, most of the salespersons that I interviewed are **not** like that. I was pleasantly surprised to find that some of the most successful salespersons do not "align" with that distorted selling style. In fact, they regard selling and what they do as a natural way of how things work and therefore they don't bring any pressure in doing that activity. The way they sell is like a *dance* – there is no pressure present, neither on the client, nor on themselves. The process is flowing, exactly because it is allowed to. They know that the moment they bring pressure and neediness into the mix, the flowing stops.

Moreover, it was another *distinction* that hit me when interviewing successful salespersons: they think of *selling* (as activity, as a concept) as **separate** from *buying*. That is, selling is selling and buying is buying. *Selling* is what the salesperson does, and *buying* is what the client does. When they think of *selling*, that doesn't mean that the client *has to buy!*

Most – if not all – sales managers and salespersons consider that if the client did not buy, this means that "the salesperson didn't sell"; it means they didn't do their job, they didn't do what they were supposed to do.

But what if the successful salespersons that I interviewed got it right? What if *selling* does not mean that the client *must* buy (although this is the *desired outcome*, and they may very well do so)?

There are many examples in life, where the *process* and the desired *outcome* (which is flowing from that process) are distinct. One can say that one is "doing the *process*", even if the "*desired outcome*" is not yet produced:

- A person can "hunt" even if they don't kill any prey that day. They can honestly say that they "have been hunting", especially if the activity was intended as *play*.

- The same goes for "fishing" – a person "has been fishing" although they didn't catch any fish.

- A person can "play" a game even if they don't win, although they want that. When you play pool with your friends, of course you'd like to win – but you still "played", even if you didn't win.

- A person "prays" even if their desire is not granted by the gods. No comments needed here.

- A person can say that they "made an offering" even if their offering was not accepted.

Similarly, a person "sells" even if the exchange is not accepted and does not take place.

In Chapter 14 "Let's reinvent *selling* together" I'll put all this in a form that you could use.

Up to this point I wanted to draw your attention on "the problem": how it appears, how it manifests and how it perpetuates, as a natural consequence of the current understanding of what selling means.

What is the problem I am referring to?

The fact that many salespersons feel uncomfortable with their profession (trying to disguise it under various names) and, as a result, they are *incongruent* about what they do. This incongruence transpires in their behavior, so the clients become [unconsciously] suspicious and refrain from buying. Perhaps the salespersons will even stop selling altogether, in order to stop the uncomfortable feeling. In the end, nobody wins.

Now I'd like to introduce to you a different understanding of this concept, without imposing it as "the truth" or implying that you "should" adopt it. Rather, I suggest that you try it on, wholeheartedly, and notice how you feel about yourself as a salesperson and about selling, in general, as a result. Notice what happens to "the problem". Can you still create it, even if you try hard?

PART. 2:

NEW PARADIGM FOR SELLING

The issue is not about the salesperson, but rather about the way they sell.

And the way people sell is always **in coherence with their** understanding **of what selling means.**

I called this Part "new paradigm", but it's a misnomer. In actuality it's only a revitalization of the original model of selling, the way people understood it and practiced it thousands of years ago.

CHAPTER 10:

Etymology

"When you change the way you describe something, when you change the way you talk or think about something, you change the results that you get."
John Grinder

What is Etymology?

The dictionary gives us this definition: "It is the study of the origin and historical development of a linguistic form by determining its basic elements, earliest known use, and changes in form and meaning, tracing its transmission from one language to another, identifying its cognates in other languages"

In plain language, etymology shows us the origins of a particular word, what was its meaning the first time it was used and the transformations of that meaning over time.

In Chapter 4. "What is Selling, according to the contemporary paradigm?" we learned from the language historian Anne Curzan that words shift their meaning over time, keeping up with the popular usage.

We have also noted that, for the most part, the current meaning of the concept of selling is not all that useful: there is a social label for salespersons (and for *selling* in general) loaded with stereotypes that are not that appreciative. The salespersons are implicitly pressured to adopt those stereotypes through labeling and that creates a lot of tension and conflict in their psyche. They want that pressure to stop, so they stop selling, altogether.

So, it's not the word or the concept that creates the problem, but the *meaning* that a community holds for it. You see, a word is only a symbol, a representation of something. So, the question is, what is that "something" that you want to call *selling*?

Instead of "making up" a new meaning and risking all sorts of endless arguments, I researched the origins of the concept of *selling*. So let's see how old this concept is and what was people's understanding of it in the past. Perhaps you'll be surprised to notice that it's well-known to the salespersons and recognized in the sales literature – but it's only contemplated superficially, at the 'form' level, not at the 'essence' level.

CHAPTER 11:

What Did People Originally Understand by Selling?

"Alone we can do so little; together we can do so much."
Helen Keller

I was amazed to find out that the concept of *selling* is thousands of years old. Here there are a few examples of how the word was used back then:

- In Proto-Germanic language (spoken about 2000-2500 years ago), "saljana" meant "to offer", "to give";

- In Gothic language (spoken starting around year 400), "saljan" meant "to offer a sacrifice" or "to cause to take";

- In Old English, or Anglo-Saxon (spoken starting around year 500), "sellan" meant "to give", "to grant", "to hand over", "to deliver";

- In Latin, "consilium" meant "to give advice".

As a matter of fact, *selling* was not used in association with money. The meaning of "selling" as "giving up for money" emerged only around year 1000!

The meaning of "selling" as "deceiving" appeared only in 1600's.

The phrase "hard sell", overused today as a generalization, was first recorded on 1952!

Now you have a glimpse over the meaning shift of the concept of selling, the way people's understanding of it evolved over centuries.

It was interesting for me to realize that "sell" has the same origin as the word "counsel" – a term that lawyers and doctors happily adopt, while distancing themselves from the term of "selling".

Let's take a look at some common meanings of the word "counsel":

- Something that provides direction or advice as to a decision or course of action.

- To recommend; to give advice.

- The act of exchanging opinions and ideas; consultation.

- Advice, guidance, opinion - especially as solicited from a knowledgeable person; to consult with an expert.

- Discussion, especially on future procedure; a plan of action.

- Consultation; deliberation.

- Wisdom; prudence.

We can easily recognize that "counsel" is a compound word: "con" + "sel".

The only difference between "counseling" and "selling" is the prefix "con", which means "with" or "together".

Since the act of "giving" (see the original meaning of "selling") implies that more than one person is involved in the activity (i.e., there is one who gives and one who receives), I don't see that prefix as a differentiation between the named concepts. Rather, I see it as a reinforcement of the idea that both activities presuppose the *cooperation* between the persons involved.

Thus, we have a more complete image for the meaning of the word "selling":

to give, to offer, while having *the agreement* of the other person to receive.

Another meaning of selling that caught my attention was "**to cause to take**"...

Think of this for a moment...

When one would *not* want to *take* a gift that somebody offers to them?

When *you* would be wary of accepting someone's gift?

It's when you *don't trust* them, when you *don't feel safe and secure* in their presence, when you have reasons to believe that they have *ulterior motives, a hidden agenda* for giving you that gift. In other words, when that gift is "about *them*", not really "about *you*".

Good to keep in mind when you think about going out and "sell somebody"...

CHAPTER 12:

The Most Fascinating Side of the Original Sense of Selling

"Science is not only compatible with spirituality; it is a profound source of spirituality."
Carl Sagan

What's even more captivating is the fact that *selling* was frequently used in religious contexts (in accordance with the few texts available from those old times). When people were going to the temples with *offerings* and *sacrifices*, they were **selling** those offerings to the gods!

Now, let's think for a moment about the background implications of this aspect:

- Going to the temple it's a *ritual*. There is a proper time and a proper way to do it – and that "appropriateness" is dictated by the gods. In other words, I need to have gods' *permission* before going to their temple and making an offering.

  - Zoom in on selling today – I observed that some salespersons carry a sense of entitlement in regards to people's attention and to people's option of having a conversation or not. They behave as if everybody is somehow obligated to stop whatever they are doing, just to talk with them. Have you ever had this experience: you are walking around, thinking your own thoughts and, all of a sudden, you are startled by this enthusiastic salesperson who starts to tell you about all the wonderful things they can do for you? There was no consideration, no respect for your time and energy? Simply because they happened to see you, now you are obligated to give *them* your attention - because *they want* it! How does that make you feel?

- Many other salespersons, on another hand, are reluctant to make *any* contact at all, because they fear that they will be considered an "interruption".

  - Well, yes, you *are* an "interruption", but only until you are not! That is, "interrupt" them to ask for their *permission* to talk to them (just as if you were to ask them for directions when you got lost in a new city). If they say "no", then it's all good; you would've never had their attention anyway (I hope you realize that if you simply start talking to somebody , that doesn't mean that they are actually listening to you!).

    o However, if they say "yes", then you are *not anymore* an "interruption"!

- The *attitude* that I would have when going to a temple is one of *presence, respect* and *consideration*.

  o Zoom in on selling today – What if your focus, as a salesperson, were to enter the sales interaction with an attitude of *presence* and *connection*? An attitude of deep *respect* for that prospect? There would be no room for *arrogance, pressure* or *manipulation*. How would this change the dynamic of that interaction?

- I would bring to the temple the **gods'** preferred sacrifices (that is, I am not bringing my leftovers or worthless stuff from my stable, but *what **they** value*), with the attitude that I *will continue* to bring more of the same. That means that those sacrifices are not a "one time deal", but rather an *experience* of the *value* that I am *willing to continue to give them.*

  o Zoom in on selling today – people don't buy things, but they buy things that they *value* – and only when *they* consider that the value they need to "give up" is less than the value they "receive". But, in order for someone to realize that there is *value* in a certain product, **they need to have an *experience* of that** - they need to "*evaluate*" what their life would be like, *with or without* that product! This *experience* that I give to my prospect is "my offering".

  o The alternative that's mostly used today is to lure the prospect into believing in a perceived value that would exist in that product, to tell them whatever they want to hear in order to "push the sale", to promise them results beyond their dreams or to scare them with the bad consequences of not buying. How appropriate would those tactics appear in the context of 'temples' and 'gods'?

  o Salespersons want people to buy their products, but instead of allowing the person to have a real *experience* of their product - so to properly evaluate it on their own - their thinking goes towards "how to *convince* and *persuade* this person *to like* my product", "how to *increase their desire*" or "how to *get them to buy*".

○ Their focus is on how to "*get* something *from* the client", instead of "how to *give* something *for* the client". The sales process turns to be *about the salesperson* and their agenda, instead of making it *about the client* and their satisfaction.

○ When you give the person a genuine *experience of your offering*, they will know for a fact what they will *receive* in working with you and they will know exactly if your *offer* has *value* for them or not.

- If they don't value your product, then you don't want them as a client (because a dissatisfied client will consume you more time and energy than the profit you made from that sale, so it's worthless. If you "convince" or "manipulate" them to buy, they will not *own* that decision; at the first little mishap, they will hold *you* responsible and they will punish you).

- But if they *do* value what you offer and it is *their own* decision to go ahead and buy it, then you'll know that they will wholeheartedly defend and protect that *exchange of value*. They will make it work, because now *they own* their *decision*. It's the *commitment and consistency principle* at work, in a good way.

• When I give my offerings to the gods, I need to do that wholeheartedly, with a 'clean heart'. I need to be "Abel", not "Cain".

○ Zoom in on selling today – the purpose most salespersons get in contact with people is to see if they can "make a sale". They use people and the "giving" as *means to a personal end.* If this is their inner attitude, no matter how cleverly they try to disguise it, people will sense it – sooner or later. Their offering is not given with a "clean heart" and it will not be well-received.

● I am going to the temples to *ask* the gods for something (health, peace, food, whatever), but I don't *demand* it. Prayer is a *dialogue* with the gods - a conversation, if you wish. I carry *no sense of entitlement.* However, although I have no guarantees that my desire would become true, I **know** that if I continue to wholeheartedly *offer value* to them, they will recognize my *true intention to serve* and, somehow, my wish will be granted, sooner or later, one way or another. This *offering* is only my way of *paying forward* – not with the "expectation" to receive something back, but **knowing** that I will be rewarded - simply because that's how *life* works.

○ Zoom in on selling today – what if the salesperson made an *offer, asked* for an *exchange of value,* while knowing and candidly accepting that the other party might not find as advantageous the *exchange of value* and that *no* is possible. It's not "healthy" to hold the expectation that if you *serve* someone through an *experience,* they will necessarily become your client. That expectation will make you attached to the outcome and "needy". "Needy" is not attractive; it's rather like <client repellant>.

○ *Maintain the Want and Let go of the Need.* Can you Want

something, without Needing it?

○ You *will* have clients if you serve people by *giving them an experience of your offer* – perhaps not **this** person, but you *will*.

CHAPTER 13:

What Principles Can We Gather from the Original Sense of Selling

"Effective leadership is putting first things first. Effective management is discipline, carrying it out."
Stephen R. Covey

Let's put together the "zoom-in" *guidelines* that we extracted above. We'll refine them in the next chapters. But, for now, we have:

1. Become *present, connect* with yourself and your environment.

   a) Stop feeding with energy all of those Ego's stories that keep running in your mind.

   b) Set an *intention* (not "expectation") of what you want to have happen. Then forget about it – focus exclusively 'on them'.

2. Connect with the person you're talking to. *Go First* into a state of *presence*.

3. IF they acknowledge that they have a *problem* (something they want to be different in their life) *ask for permission to give them an experience* of your possible *solution*.

4. *Give them an experience* so that they can note for

themselves if your *solution* has *value* for them. Make the process "about them", not "about *you* and what *you* want". Focus on "*serving* them", "*giving* something *for* them", instead of "*getting* something *from* them". Make it real and hold nothing back – focus on *serving* their True Authentic Self, not on *pleasing* their Ego.

5. Ask for what you want; not from a place of entitlement or expectation, nor from one of a beggar. Rather, from a place of equal status, *knowing* that if what you have is *valuable* to them and the proposed exchange is fair, they will go for it.

    a) Allow them to *own* their decision. *Let go of the need* for them to say *yes*. Be candid, maintain your innocence and equanimity in regards to their response.

    b) If they *don't find value in your offer*, you don't become "needy". They may come back later or they may refer someone else to you. Remain *present*, believing in the power of your *Intention*.

Note – these are principles deducted from the religious usage of the concept of selling. I'll complete the image of this list on a future chapter, by adapting it to the actual selling process.

As you look at these *principles*, how do you sense *selling* now? How does it feel to you?

What difference can you spot on your willingness to go ahead and sell your thing to your prospects, realizing that what you do is actually *offering* them value, with their permission and in a candid manner?

What difference can you sense, knowing that *selling* doesn't need to be something hard, tough or an activity in which the salesperson puts a lot of effort in "making" the other person buy?

Can you imagine selling without the need to *persuade* someone to do something against their will (even if you believe it will be good for them)?

Can you imagine *selling by giving an experience* to a person who gave you *permission* to demonstrate your *solution*? What would that be like for you?

I know that some of you might have a hard time adjusting your perspective and making sense of *selling* the way I describe it. Many of the people I interviewed had the same experience. They uttered a lot of "yes, but..." statements, trying to bring coherence and to make sense of all of the elements of their stories about what selling is or it should be.

What if we were allowed to reinvent the concept of selling, together? Let's play with this for a moment.

CHAPTER 14:

Let's Reinvent Selling Together

"As we make and keep commitments, even small commitments, we begin to establish an inner integrity that gives us the awareness of self-control and the courage and strength to accept more of the responsibility for our own lives. By making and keeping promises to ourselves and others, little by little, our honor becomes greater than our moods."
Stephen R. Covey

Let's start by agreeing on something. Selling is important. Selling is actually vital. Can you imagine a place, a country, a community where nobody sells anything to anybody? A place where no *selling* takes place, whatsoever? How quickly do you estimate that this community will extinguish altogether? (I know I said this before, but it is worth repeating, since so many people assert that *selling* is a bad thing).

Value grows only when it is *exchanged*. A place where no *exchange of value* takes place is a place where *value* doesn't grow. And, what doesn't grow, shrinks, diminishes and eventually disappears.

If that's the case, if *selling* is a necessary part of *life*, can you at least *consider the possibility* that *Nature* also conceived a harmonious and congruent manner of *selling*? It did it for so many other essential and vital things - so it *must* be a way to *sell* that is enjoyable and pleasant.

To Act Congruently

If the current paradigm of *selling* makes you feel *anxious, incongruent* and *unattractive*, I don't blame you. I feel the same. The *"selling steps"* that you may have learned about are treating the client as if people are machines: do this, do that, find their needs, gather intelligence, handle their objections, close them and so forth.

There are many techniques that are taught (and I used to love using them). However, did it ever happen to you to "apply" a technique and it felt so awkward that everybody could tell from a mile away that you were fake? That technique worked fantastically well for your trainer and, perhaps, for your colleague, but not for you.

Why is that?

Because *they* are not *you*.

Go briefly to the end of the book and find Glossary of Terms. Take a quick look at the "Congruent vs Incongruent" definition. It's important.

When your internal *values* and *beliefs*, your *inner understandings* are not in alignment with your *behavior*, then you'll act *incongruently*, as a bad actor. Nobody will believe you, nobody will trust you and nobody will "play" with you.

If that technique worked beautifully for somebody else, it's probably because their values were aligned with the behavior (i.e., words, tone of voice, physiology) required in that technique. Since it didn't work for you, it's probably because your values are different than theirs.

I suggest that the most important thing is to be capable to **sell congruently**. Your outer actions will have to be *harmoniously* aligned with your inner understanding of the process, so you can feel true to yourself. It is only then that you'll be able to feel good about *selling* and to *cultivate* beautiful relationships with people who will want to buy from you.

That's exactly the reason why I spent so much time until now explaining the distinctions within the *original* paradigm of *selling*, the religious usage, the etymology and other related concepts – to help you build new and more harmonious understandings and considerations about what selling *could mean*, which will serve you better, allowing you to *sell congruently*.

How I Understand Selling

This is my understanding of what *selling* is:

Selling is the *process* of **connecting** with a person, noting if they **admit** to having a **problem** for which they want a **solution now,** *asking for* **permission** and **offering** an **experience** of your solution to that problem and – if they find **value** in your solution - making a **proposal** for an **exchange of value.**

Let me say it again:

Selling is a *process*:

- It is the ongoing activity, not a static outcome - it is not about the end result of it.

95

Selling is the process where:

- I *connect* (instead of shallowly "build a relationship") with a person;

- If they acknowledge having a *problem* and desiring a *solution now*, I ask for *permission* to *offer them an experience* of my *solution* to their *problem*;

- I give them that experience, allowing them to *directly feel* the *value* of my solution;

- If they find *value* in what I have, I make a *proposal for an exchange of value.*

In other words, during the entire process, from *prospecting* to *agreement*, my focus is on:

- *being present* so that I can *connect* with them;

- noticing if the person *acknowledges* a *problem* to which they want a *solution now*;

- *asking permission* and *offering* them an *experience* of my *solution*;

- *asking* for an *exchange of value* (if my *solution* is *valuable* to them).

Please note that I didn't say anything about their chosen response of accepting my proposal or not. That would refer to *buying*, and that's *their* part. It does not belong to the *selling* activity, just as the gods' response to one's prayer is not included as part of the prayer itself.

Let's consider the details of this *process*, starting from the Golden Rule (see Glossary of Terms) and from the notes on the Chapter

12 "The most fascinating side of the *original* sense of *selling*". I'll describe the way I view the process of *selling* and its unfolding. Note if that makes a difference in your attitude towards it:

- "Prospecting" – I'll elaborate more on this in a separate chapter. In short, *prospecting* is about *connecting with a human being*. This is where my focus is – to *offer* and *initiate a connection*. I don't even think of them as "prospects" – I let go of any agenda of "getting something *from* them". I simply start a conversation with somebody, with a human being. I *connect* with them. I learn about them. If – and I emphasize IF – they mark out that they have a *problem* to which I might have a *solution*, then I ask questions to find out more. However, sometimes time is of the essence, so I could *ask directly* if they experience such *problem* and if *solving it now* would be valuable to them.

  o Things that I look for:

    ▪ Do they *overtly* admit that this is a *problem* for them?

    ▪ Do they *overtly* admit that they want a *solution* to that?

    ▪ Do they *overtly* admit that they want that solution *now*?

  o If they say *no* to *any* of the above qualifications, then I have no business continuing *selling* to them - especially when I *know* that they *do* have that problem. If they don't admit having it or if they minimize the importance of solving it, this only shows that they put little value on me and on my solution. They are implicitly telling me that they are not committed to solving that problem. Moreover, if I insist and "convince" them to meet with me, my status just dropped and my offer devalued.

- I might ask them if they know somebody else who may need my *solution*. Since I "proved" that my main focus is in *offering a connection* (rather than pushing for what <I> want), they will be more likely to refer me to somebody they know.

  o If they say yes to all of the above qualifications, I *offer* to *give them an experience* of my *solution*.

- If they accept it, I facilitate for them that *experience*: this is the "presentation" that salespersons do for their products, the "test drive" of that car, the food sample in the store, the "coaching experience" session that you offer, and so forth.

  o I do my best to turn that "presentation" into an "experience", rather than me telling them empty words about why <I> think that they should buy my thing.

- At the end of it, if they found *value* in that (I either ask them or I notice their reactions), I make an *offer* for an *exchange of value*. I tell them the *value* I want in return for the *value* they want from me. It's not necessary to justify the *value* that I ask; it's their job to compare the *value* they should give with the *value* that they get.

  o If they consider the *value* they have to *give* to be smaller than the *value* they *receive*, then I see no reason why they should not agree with the exchange. You note that there is no need for *handling objections*, convincing, persuasion or manipulation in all this process.

o If they find the value they have to give to be larger than the value they would receive, then there's no point in me convincing them of anything. No sane person would ever go for an exchange where they would lose value!

- However, there is a mental mechanism that's going on in the process of comparing values - I'll talk about it in Chapter 19 "About Value and Exchange of Value". I'll also point ways of ethically influencing that comparison – that is, in ways that I would accept to be done onto myself!

Do you see any pressure whatsoever in this process? Is there any "convincing", "manipulation" or "deceiving" anywhere?

Do any of those "points" conflict with your beliefs and values or with the harmonious nurturing of relationships? Is it possible for you to remain congruent while going through the "phases" of this process?

If you were approached in this manner by a salesperson, how would that selling experience feel for you? Would you feel respected and appreciated, safe and secure, allowed to make your own decisions?

Now that we defined selling as a general concept, let's go a step forward and define the purpose of selling in business.

CHAPTER 15:

What Is, Really, the Purpose of Selling in Business?

*"I don't wish to be everything to everyone,
but I would like to be something to someone."*
Javan

Most people would probably say that the purpose of a business is to make money. It makes sense, in a way, but when you look deeper, it doesn't. If that was true, then a "bank robber" would be 'doing a business'.

So, clearly, a qualification is required. If you compare the companies that thrived with the ones that failed, the main difference you'll find is that the former ones focused on *giving value* to their clients, while the later focused on *taking value*.

As Bob Marley used to sing: "You can fool some people sometimes, but you can't fool all the people all the time."

Thus, let's propose that:

The purpose of a business is to offer a fair exchange of value to their clients.

That means that:

- The company *offers* something (a *product* or *service*) to the prospects;

- The prospects find that particular "something" to be

valuable to them – it solves a *problem* that they have;

○ An important thing to keep in mind is that *value* is *always* in the eyes of the client. If the client doesn't find that "something" to be *valuable*, then it is not, regardless of the salesperson's opinion;

● The company asks for an *exchange of value*. Most often, it puts a monetary number on that *value* that's provided to the client, as a 'representation' for the *value* that the company wants in return. If the client considers that the *value* they *receive* is more than the *value* they *give*, then there is no reason why they should not go ahead with the *exchange*;

● Since the client felt respected, appreciated and given the liberty to decide for themselves if the *exchange* is fair to them, they will come back, *buying* again and again, and recommending the company to their friends.

> *"The goal is not to do business with everybody who needs what you have. The goal is to do business with people who believe what you believe."*
> *Simon Sinek*

With that, I think we outlined the main building blocks that make up the meaning of selling. In the next chapters, I'll put arrange them in a way that will introduce to you *selling* as a 'heart to heart' activity.

PART. 3:

WHAT IS "HEART TO HEART (H2H) SELLING"

Selling is the process of **connecting** with a person, asking for **permission** and **offering** an **experience** of your solution to a problem they **admit** having and making a **proposal** for an **exchange of value.**

or, more directly:

Selling is the *process* where I **connect** with a person, I note if they **admit** having a **problem** to which they want a **solution now**, I **ask for permission** and I **offer** them an **experience** of my solution to their problem and – if they find **value** in my solution – I make a **proposal** for an **exchange of value.**

"Heart to Heart Selling" hinges on some key concepts. In the next chapters, I will explore those concepts and some subtle distinctions about them, because I believe this will bring more clarity and will solidify the idea that I intend to build.

CHAPTER 16:

H2H Selling Is Centered on and Starts with Fostering a Connection

"I Know that service Always comes back – I just can't be attached to coming back from the same person."
- somebody -

Most of the sales models that I found *talk* about *creating relationships*, indeed.

However, there are two aspects that I want to point out about some of those sales models.

First – the "creating of a relationship" is mentioned only as a secondary focus, after prospecting or approaching the prospect. Some models talk about relationships only *after* the closing step!

However, the funny part is that *all* sales models tell you to ask the prospect all sorts of questions, with the assumption that the prospect will answer to you, honestly and openly. As a salesperson, you're supposed to start talking to the prospect, ask [leading] questions, uncover their needs and values, handle objections... But, if the prospect *doesn't want* to answer to your inquiries or if they answer only perfunctory, without engaging, then you have nothing. If you don't have their *attention* and *engagement*, you have nothing!

In other words, there must be something that needs to happen BEFORE you can start asking those questions.

Second, they talk about "creating and managing relationships" as if people were some mechanical devices!

Think of this for a moment...

How would you feel if you were to learn that your romantic partner "created" and that they are actively "managing" the relationship they have with you?

I think of a *relationship* the same way as I think of a *flower*. How can you "manage" a flower? A flower "happens" when you remove the restrictions that prevent it from "happening". The presupposition is that the flower "wants" to grow and you can only facilitate the conditions for it to grow, all by itself, by removing the hindrances.

You don't "build" a relationship by using a hammer and nails, but by planting a seed and creating the conditions for that seed to emerge on its own.

The same goes for *love*.

Yes, I agree, you could labor a relationship using superficial appearances and acting as to make-believe. But this would be superficial. Superficial is also insubstantial, and a relationship that's not based on substance is not a real relationship.

A Basic Ingredient for a Relationship to Emerge

Here's one important thing that prevents a relationship from "happening": the lack of trust. For the prospect to open up to a relationship with you and to fully and honestly engage in the conversation with you, they need to feel *safe and secure* in your presence.

Think of this for a moment...

Let's turn tables for a change. Humans are social creatures. Generally speaking, people are open and eager to develop new relationships. How would *you* like it to be, for you? If you were to meet somebody or if someone were to approach you, what would need to happen for you to agree to a relationship with that person?

Review for a moment the Exercise/ Experience at the end of Chapter 8, Sub-Chapter "Your Understanding of what Selling means".

What would be your gut reaction to their approach if you feel them as *needy,* as *manipulative,* as wanting something to *get from* you, using all sorts of leading questions? Would you feel *safe and secure* as to open up and *play* with them or would you feel wary of answering their questions, out of fear of being cornered?

My guess is that - if you're like most people in this world - you won't like to start a relationship with someone who only wants something *from* you. So, why on earth would you expect others to behave differently? No wonder most salespersons are walking around frustrated that nobody wants to talk to them!

Let Go of the Need to Make the Sale

What would happen if you were to take out and *let go of that need* to make the sale?

Yes, you *want* to make it happen. That's your *intention*, and that's OK.

Can you Want something, without Needing it?

What if you were to realize that holding the *need* to make the sale is the very cause of it *not* happening?

How would you think, feel and behave if you were to "forget" about the sale, about your sales manager, about your quota or about your bills - just for a while, as you start talking to this person in front of you? What happens as you put your entire focus on them, on who they are, as a person, just to understand them as a human being? Obviously, if they decide to not talk to you, you are OK with that, too, because you respect them and appreciate them, as they are, as a human being – not from an attitude of *superiority* or *condescension*, but from an attitude of *compassion*, realizing that they must've been through some tough experiences that eroded their trust in people. Give them *space*, allow them to know you first, if they so desire. *Trust* is given, not demanded! They will give it to you when you *give it first*!

Focus solely on *connecting* with them. *Connection* is not something that you *do* or *create*, but rather something that you *allow* to happen and *become aware* of, when both of you are *present in the moment*.

Look at them as if they are your *best friend* and you have only their good-ness at heart. There's nothing you want **from** them, but you'd like to make a gift **for** them - only to the extent that they want it.

Obviously, you know that for a gift to be valuable, it needs to be *accepted* (that is, not forced). Also, you know that if you give a gift even with the *slightest need* of getting something in return, that cancels out the notion of "gift", turning it into "manipulation". Your motivation for the giving should be *in the giving*, in and of itself. You cannot use the gift as a means to an end. You cannot have an ulterior motive for doing this. When you are *present*, the *past* and the *future* are irrelevant. Only the *present moment* matters, what happens now between you and the person you're talking to.

Mother Teresa said "It's not how much we give but how much love we put into giving."

Give *for the sake of giving* – it will make you feel good about yourself. Pay forward – knowing that it *will* come back to you, sooner or later, from one person or from another. Give as if you're giving 'to the Universe', not to 'this person'. Give knowing that 'the Universe' is always paying back when given wholeheartedly.

Just as in 'prayer' – if one goes to the temple and gives one's offerings to the gods solely out of some extrinsic motivation, with a sense of expectation and entitlement, then one would be like Cain and one's gifts would be rejected by the gods. One can *want* something from the gods, but one cannot *demand* that. The *demanding* points out that the *want* turned into a *need* and the person has an *attachment* to the end result.

Think of this for a moment...

The *want* has turned into a *need* if I feel any resentment if it

doesn't happen...

Remove any touch of *superiority* or *condescension* when making that gift, because the person in front of you will feel *patronized*. The gift will then become only a cunning way for you to sustain the idea of your own superiority or higher status. The gift will be 'about you', not 'about them'.

What gift to give?

The Gift of Your Presence and Connection

Well, let's think for a moment, what do people crave the most? My experience tells me that the sweetest gift, that you could **always** give to someone and that people will **always** appreciate is your **full attention, presence, understanding** and **acceptance**. People want to be understood and listened to, deeply and genuinely, but they rarely give that to others. Be one of the few in their lives who truly *listens* to them and truly wants to *understand* them as a human being!

> *"The greatest gift you can give another is the purity of your attention."*
> *Richard Moss*

Think of this for a moment...

Have you ever talked to a friend and they were continuously giving you advice of what you should've done or what you should do, patronizing you for your naivety, without any intention to understand you first? How did that go, how did that make you feel?

We all want *acceptance* and *understanding*, although we mostly realize that when we don't have it (that's how we realize the *value* of something, actually). So, Go First and *give* it first, if you want to receive it at your turn. *Give* what you want to *receive*; not from an attitude of *expecting* to receive, but one of *knowing* that you *will* receive it – perhaps not from this person, but it will come from somebody else.

Connection "happens" when you and your client are together *present in the moment,* including each other in each own awareness and focusing on the same idea.

Note: I put quotes around "happens" because *connection* is something that already exists, all the time, among us. It's just that we are not aware of this aspect of life, because we are *thinking ourselves out of it.* When we slow down and become *present,* that *connection* has room to show up in our awareness. And that's when *magic* happens.

Experience/ Exercise

Let's practice this attitude of *presence* when talking with somebody.

I will presume that you're not reading this book while driving or handling machineries... if you are, you know what to do: stop that and focus exclusively on this exercise.

Sit down for a moment, if you weren't already. Get comfortable, keep your spine straight and put your hands on your thighs. Take a couple of deep breaths, then close your eyes and continue paying attention to your regular breathing. Follow that air entering your lungs and then going out through your nostrils. Count ten complete breaths, noticing where do you feel most comfortable in your body. When you're done, open your eyes.

Make a phone call to a friend and just *be present*. Ask questions, but not with the purpose of "leading" them in a particular direction or to "make" them think or do something. Just be curious about them, the way you'd like for someone to be genuinely curious and interested in you.

If you notice that you become slightly irritated because they don't agree with you, because they don't unconditionally accept your idea or maybe because they say something you disagree with – oops, *stop* it! Realize you started to "judge". Look **at** that "judging thought" and *allow it to pass.* Remember that your purpose is solely to "observe" the other person, to find out who they are, what they think and feel. Just as a scientist is "observing" and learning about its object of study – there's no judgment, only curiosity.

And, when you can witness your "judging thoughts" and let them pass, notice a serenity and peacefulness that starts to develop inside of you. Memorize that state and recall it before starting a selling conversation.

CHAPTER 17:

About Presence

"Most people do not listen with the intent to understand; they listen with the intent to reply."
Stephen R. Covey

Human beings rarely live in the *present moment*. Their mind is always busy comparing what happens *now* with something similar that happened in their *past*, in order to give them a quick way to handle it. It's a good tool to have, because it saves time and energy: if it rains, you'll know you better take your umbrella, because otherwise the rain will soak you (as it happened once...).

Similarly, once a person has labeled you as a "salesperson", now they revivify all of their memories about their past selling experiences with other "salespersons". Or, if you start telling them about your product or service, their mind will instantly bring up their previous knowledge about it – which may be more or less accurate. But now they are judging all that you say and do through that filter. The information that "fits" their previous knowledge will go through and will be accepted, while the information that "doesn't fit" what they think they know will be rejected.

If there is any discrepancy between what you say and what their inner voice tells them, who do you think they will believe: you or themselves?

In other words, they will only hear what they already know. We *all* do this – even you, while reading these lines. If you didn't already know this mechanism, you'll dispute this idea: "No, it can't be true. I am not like this. This is not what happens..."

Think of this for a moment...

Have you ever talked with somebody who had a certain issue that bothered them, for which you knew the answer (because it worked for you and for others), but they simply wouldn't even consider your solution? They kept telling you "No, that wouldn't work, I just know it. I couldn't do it. I thought of that already." They cannot hear you.

When someone goes through an emotion that they cannot manage properly – perhaps a tragic event just happened or perhaps they just won the lottery – they cannot hold themselves together. Their mind is running a hundred miles per hour, all over the place: they start an idea, then they jump immediately to a different thought, then something else catches their attention. They ask you something and, without even listening to your answer, they ask you the same thing seconds later...

Even if you didn't live directly these experiences, perhaps you saw movies where this situation was painted. What does the hero do in order to help this "hysterical" person get back together? Maybe they slap him, they shake him by the shoulders or yell at him. Or, maybe after a while, when that person's mind got exhausted from that much agitation, they calmed down all by themselves. You may see that person grabbing the back of a chair, lean on the wall or pinch themselves.

What happens there?

Their mind struggles like a restless horse, trying to make sense of what just happened. It runs in their *past* and because it doesn't find any *reference experience* from which to collect the answer, it keeps looking, running back and forth, browsing through years of personal history. Then, when a shock happens (e.g., the slapping) they finally calm down and **become present**, they start considering that situation **as it is, for what it is**, fresh and anew, without searching for any patterns into which to fit it. When they connect with something that happens in the *present moment* (e.g., touching the wall or feeling the pain of pinching) they will *become present* themselves. People instinctively know that.

What Does That Have to Do with Selling?

I wanted to make you aware that there is no point in talking to a person if that person is not listening to you, but to their voice from inside. Thus, from the very beginning, before starting a conversation with somebody, you need to focus on *facilitating for them to become present*, on their own (because you cannot "make" them become present).

Why? Because when people are **not** in the *present*, they are **not** *with you*, nor *with what you are saying*. They are *comparing* what **is** with what **was.**

You want them, when they look at you, to see **you**, rather than God-knows-what-kind of salesperson they had the mischance to talk to in their past.

You want them, when they look at your product, to see and evaluate **your product**, rather than God-knows-what-kind of cheap replica they had the bad luck to purchase in their past and broke in two days.

You see, when I *sell* something, I am not interested in "convincing" them about the benefits of my product. I am interested in *giving them an* **experience** *of my product.* It is only then that they can truly *evaluate* it, find value in it and *own* the decision to buy it. But, for them to *actually have* that experience, they need to *engage* and *be present* and *think of* what is happening *now*, as if it was for the *first time in their lives* they met a salesperson or a product like mine. Without their *engagement*, there's no *experience.* It's only an absent witnessing.

If they are *not present*, I am merely providing them an opportunity to remember noxious past experiences as a filter through which to judge me and my product.

How to Facilitate for Someone to Become Present

Obviously, I am not at all implying that you should slap or pinch the person you're talking to. Luckily enough, these are not the only ways to facilitate for someone to *become present.* I'll suggest a few ways that you could try on:

- The best way is to **Go First** – **you** *be present* before starting the conversation and, whatever happens, *remain present,* true to yourself and to your values. Your state of *presence* will influence them to become *present,* too;

- Do or say something **they don't expect** or something that doesn't fit in the stereotype they try to fit you in. Anything at all, as long as it doesn't compromise the relationship;

  ○ e.g., when you go to a car dealership, you probably

expect that a salesperson will quickly come towards you, greet you with a large smile and give you some cheap pleasantries or some leading questions. What if they come towards you, but, instead of all that, they apologize that they cannot talk to you right now, because they have a report to finish or an agreement to sign. However, they will be free in 5 minutes and, IF you will want to talk to them, you just say so. Then, they vanish.

o How would that go for you? Would that make your mind go in circles for a bit, trying to make sense of what happens? Do you start to think that *maybe* this salesperson *could* be *different* than what you assumed?

- Use **pauses** when you talk. Give them time to think and to consider your words;

- Look at them **meaningfully,** not just quickly glimpse over their head. If you're on the phone, **slow down** your agitation and allow your voice, your intonation and energy to become meaningful;

- **Let go of your need** *that they buy* – this, again, it doesn't mean that you don't **want** them to; only that you *don't need* it. It will change the way you talk and behave. You'll allow yourself to be more **playful** and that's attractive;

- Be **Playful**; that's when *being in the game* is your reward, so you won already – if you reach the highest score, that's a bonus.

- Give them a relevant **gift.** If you offer it with a "clean heart", they will accept it and will start "exploring" it. This will make them *think* about *what happens now* and will facilitate for them to become *present*;

- **Smile**. I don't mean that "fabricated" smile, where you only open your mouth. I mean **smiling with your eyes,** with your entire face, to feel your cheeks lifting and your nostrils widening. Smile with your heart – just as if you are talking with someone you genuinely *love* deeply;

- Crack a joke. *Genuine **laughing*** is an unconscious response, it tends to bring people in the present. However, this does not mean that you have to "*make* them laugh"! That's repellant. What I mean is, if you notice something funny, mention it, with "zero expectations" for them to laugh. (Paradoxically, this will make your line ten times funnier - if it is funny at all, that is);

- ***Startle*** them with something, a magic trick or a charade or even an unexpected (although pertinent) question;

- ***Move their attention***, from where it is, to where it is not. Gently, *break their pattern of thinking*. If you notice that, for instance, they are overly concerned with the price, ask them if they intend to drive that car in the mountains (!), or how they *Feel* about the investment (in contrast with them *Digitally Reasoning* about it!). The reason for this is to help them get out of their habitual, scared type of thinking and open for them the windows towards what's possible, by making available for them a new type of fresh thinking – about what happens Now, rather than about their previous fears and worries.

- Ask them **questions** about themselves, but without prying. If you're asking yourself if it's too soon for that, then it probably is;

- Build their **attention** on *you*, as a distinct human being, different from the cultural stereotype. The way to do it is to Go First: *you* put *all* of *your attention* on *them*, accepting *them* for who they are and trying to understand *them* as an individual;

- *Engage* them with the *experience* you give them about your product. The more things you ask of them to do, to answer or to look at, the less attention they will have left for other things happening around in the environment or for other unimportant thoughts, that might tend to distract them;

- *Pace* their current experience. Talk about things that they know there are true. Direct their attention to things that are happening now.

In many ways, *to be present* is a *meditation* state that you carry with you in your day-to-day activities. It's a meditation of *awareness* and *alertness* – of *presence*, that is. It's a state of *relaxed focus* and *centered-ness*. You're not "thinking" about things or events (i.e., "comparing" what happens now with some of your past experiences); you're only *observing*, sensing *what is now*, accepting it without trying to alter it. You are relaxed, non-attached, in a "no-mind" state, although alert and attentive.

Your desire for a different state of affairs should not come from an *aversion* to the current situation, but from a *knowing* that *everything changes* anyway and you are encouraging the *natural unfolding* of things towards a certain preference. There is no shade of *need* to taint the natural flow.

Experience/ Exercise

I'll try to facilitate for you a quick experience of this state. Just for the purpose of this exercise, imagine for a moment that you are caught in *quicksand*.

(I've never been in such a situation, and I hope you haven't, neither, but maybe you've seen movies about it, as I did. You don't need to panic about the image; according to the National Geographic, one would not be "drawn under" entirely, but somehow float in that sand around waistline).

You know that if you start to shake and fret, agitate or stir, you'll go deeper into the hole. You also know that if you stay still, you'll float. The only way to have a chance of escaping is to remain calm, relaxed, still, and *geeeently-veeerrrry-veeeerrry-slooowly*, almost imperceptible, shift your arms and legs towards the safe shore. All the while, you sharpen all your senses to perceive any unpredictable reaction from the quicksand, due to your movements – so that you could stop moving if something unwanted happens. Any quick agitation will liquefy the sand and it will pull you back down again.

Similarly, when you *slow down* and quiet your mind, there will be times when you'll notice that you unwillingly started to "think" of all sorts of stories. Your mind tricked you into "thinking" about the past or about the future. You may have a tendency to become frustrated and to try to "force" your mind to stay still. But this will be the same as shaking frantically in quicksand; it will only get you deeper. The solution is to relax and *pay attention*. You don't need to "stop" your mind, just observe and pay attention to wherever it wants to go, but *without engaging* with those thoughts. Look **at** your mind and to what it is doing, without letting yourself drawn in its movement – the same way as you look at a child playing with its toys, without any tendency to get involved in that.

For exercises, tips and indications to facilitate the state of presence and mindfulness, take a look at: http://www.hearttoheartselling.com/mindfulness.html

Experience/ Exercise

Another way to get acquainted with the state of *presence* might be to focus on a 3D pictogram so to discover the concealed picture. If you look at it while in a state of *tunnel* focus (or foveal vision), you won't be able to see the hidden drawing. You need to relax your eyes into *peripheral vision* and , somehow, look "behind" that drawing. You need to start from and engage with the presumption that something *is* there, although you cannot see it *yet*. Adopt an attitude of *allowing* that 'hidden image' to emerge and hold that intention regardless of what your mind is telling you. You cannot "force" that hidden image to appear (remember the quicksand), you can only *allow* it to appear. When you get that image, enjoy and memorize the state you're in. It's a state of *presence* (or very similar, put it this way).

Rapport and Connection

I'm sure you've heard about the idea of 'creating rapport' with the prospect and perhaps you learned some techniques on how to go about it. Many NLP trainers will teach that, but only the *great* ones will tell you that 'creating rapport' is not the "be-all and end-all". They will tell you that what you're really after is *'connection'* – that warm feeling that tells you that both of you became aware of the subtle connection that [already] exists between you two.

Connection "happens" all by itself when both of you are present in the moment, focusing on each other or on the same thing.

Experience/ Exercise

Call a friend and tell them two stories:

1. One in which you do your best to *excite* them about something that happened to you. Maybe you've seen something out of the ordinary or heard someone saying an outrageous thing. But your main purpose is to *impress* your friend and to *make* them emotional.

2. One in which you tell them why you liked a certain restaurant (for instance) without **any** concern about them buying into your reasons. You are just sharing your thoughts. You feel **no need** for them to agree with you, to "like" the restaurant or to "decide" to take in your advice and to go there. You are perfectly OK, impartial, untouched, indifferent in a candid way about their possible refusal *or acceptance*. Whatever their response is, you are equal, it makes no difference to you (that's called 'equanimity'). If you notice that you "slide" into "needing" them to accept your idea, *stop!* Take a deep breath, pay full attention to it, exhale slowly, shake your head and resume the conversation from a state of *presence.*

Then ask them in which of the cases they felt more comfortable talking to you and which conversation they would've preferred to have more of. My guess is that your *need to impress* them from the first conversation made them (at least a bit) uncomfortable, and that they felt more at ease and not pressured in the second one (and, paradoxically, found that their desire to check out that restaurant was higher than in the first situation).

CHAPTER 18:

About Experience

"The only source of knowledge is experience."
Albert Einstein

"Having an Experience" refers to a "subjective experience". It is a *state*, a *feeling*, a *felt sense* in relationship with a certain thing, thought, place or event, about which we are consciously aware.

For instance, two people are looking at the sunset. Whatever each one *feels* and *pays attention* to, will construct *their own experience* of that sunset. If a person is mentally *absent*, pays *no attention* and has *no conscious feelings* about what happens, then that person cannot say that they "had an experience" about that. Most probably they felt something, but they haven't been *consciously aware* of those feelings. For them, it would be just as if it didn't happen at all.

Think about this for a moment...

Ever happened to you to watch a movie while your mind was preoccupied somewhere else? How much of an emotional recollection do you have about that movie – although you may recall some of the facts?

One needs to be *present* and *alert* in order for one to "have an experience".

Experience/ Exercise

Perhaps you looked through your windows several times today, already. But have you *paid attention* to what you were seeing? Most people look, then quickly (and unconsciously) bring labels from their *past reference experiences* and assign them to what they see. They draw a conclusion about "what is" based on what they already know it's possible and true.

Right now, step up and look outside, through the window. Watch that tree, that person crossing the street, that car, as if it is for the *first* time you have ever seen anything like that. Imagine you are a scientist coming from a different planet and you're entirely amazed by what you discover on Earth. You're curios to find out how everything works, what's all about, how does it feel like to touch or smell a particular thing. Look at that tree and imagine what it would be like to have a different color or a different shape? Can you imagine how it would feel like to touch its bark or its leaves? Can you imagine the sound that the wind makes while blowing through the leaves? Feel that sound. Try to *feel* what you *see* through your eyes, however strange it may sound.

Spend a couple of minutes doing this *mindfulness* exercise. Notice how you feel inside, what's your *felt sense* about what happened. Is this different from absently judging and labeling without actually having a sensory experience?

When you're talking with your client, their *presence* (as a concept, not their *physical* presence) will make a huge difference in their *understanding* of what you *offer* (see the Chapter 17. "About Presence").

"Giving them an experience" implies that they are *present, engaged, participating* in what happens *now* (rather than

126

remembering and bringing labels and judgments from their memories).

You need to facilitate for them to *feel the meaning* of what you show and tell them. Ask questions like "What would having that **mean** to you?" and you want them to answer *fully engaged*, not just superficially.

Remember, Going First is essential. If you want them to answer meaningfully, you need to ask the questions meaningfully. Be *present first* and hold on to that, regardless of what happens. They will eventually follow, simply because states are contagious and it feels good to be *present.*

Facilitating for the prospect to *have an experience* of what you have to offer is what makes *selling* an *art* and the salesperson a *professional.* That's *selling by giving the client an experience* of your solution. "Amateurs" are "convincing" and "persuading" or even "manipulating". They don't treat *selling* as a respectable profession. Their focus is on "I need to make the client to buy".

If you want them to respect you for what you do, you need to *respect first* what you do.

CHAPTER 19:

About Value and Exchange of Value

"Price is what you pay. Value is what you get."
Warren Buffet

What is the [economic] "value" of something? We hear it all the time: "This is a *valuable* service", "The *value* of this house is one million dollars" or "You have to provide value".

But what is "value", actually?

The dictionary describes *value* as "worth in usefulness or importance to the possessor", a "quality considered worthwhile or desirable", "relative worth or importance", "sufficiently worthwhile of someone's time, effort or interest."

Value Is a Feeling

Value is not a thing – nobody could take a picture of a "value". *Value* is the result of the process of *evaluation*, that a person makes in regards to a particular thing – just like a *decision* is the result of the process of *deciding*.

This process it's an ongoing process, it never stops.

It also looks like *value* is relative, subject to the *evaluator's* consideration. Value is a *feeling*, a personal experience. There is *no [universal] value* independent from the *evaluator*.

There are many theories about *value*. Well known economists and philosophers wrote many theories about it. They may be correct from a theoretical standpoint, but I find many of them too mechanical, not taking into consideration basic human psychology. The classical sales theory says that people don't buy *features*, they buy *benefits* – this is closer to the reality, but still gives too much credit to the rationality of the decision making process. From a simplistically practical perspective, by my experience and of the people I interviewed, people buy *feelings, states, meanings.*

In other words, people buy what those benefits *mean* to them.

All decisions are *emotional*, based on *feelings* and what things *mean* to people.

Think of this for a moment...

Everybody knows and agrees with the fact that smoking is damaging for people's health and for their finances. All logical reasons would point to a reality where nobody would smoke. And yet, what we see is different. Why? Because people make decisions based on *feelings*, not on *logic*. And they decided that smoking is making them feel good.

People make decisions based on *feelings*, not on *logic*. They perceive as *valuable* the things that bring them the *most pleasure* or the *least pain*.

Value of something has *little* to do with the abstract practical use of that something, but has *a lot* to do with how the person **feels** about what that "practical usage" **means** to them.

130

I believe that the *value* of a particular good stands in its subjective "utility" for the person making the "evaluation". From my perspective, something "has *value*" only to the extent that "it's worthwhile" *for me*; it's not necessary that other people would assign to it the same value and actually they might find it "not worthy" for themselves.

Think of this for a moment...

You own a screwdriver and that's of a great *value* to you, because you are an electrician. In your eyes, that screwdriver has a real 'practical use'. However, for me, as a coach with no technical propensities, this 'practical usage' *means* nothing, so I have *no feelings* about it. Thus, it has no *value* to me.

The *value* of something is not *intrinsic* or *objective*, but highly *subjective* to the *evaluator*/ buyer.

The reason I wanted to emphasize this is because too many times salespersons fall into their own trap, believing that what they sell is "*valuable*". It is not, until *the buyer* finds a *subjective* use of it (e.g., *solving a problem* they experience). If you, as a salesperson, still operate from this "intrinsic value" perspective, I encourage you to observe how it causes you frustration when someone refuses your offer. Why does this happen? Because such perspective implies that *everybody* should recognize the *value* in that product you sell - and that's not possible.

I can see how this belief might empower you, to some extent, in motivating you to go out and promote your product. However, when you accept that *value* it's a dynamic concept and it always sits in the eyes of the 'evaluator', you'll feel more free to show your product to more people without any "expectation" of approval and you'll avoid unnecessary frustration. You'll eliminate the *need* and you'll become *more attractive* as a conversation partner.

In a way, you don't "offer *value*"; you're offering a "thing" and its possible benefits and, if *they* feel *value* in it and if they want it (e.g., because it solves a *problem* they experience), you may ask for an *exchange of value.*

Deconstructing the Concept of Value

The way I see it, there are two parts to *value*:

1. If it exists or not - How do you know that something is *valuable* to you, **at all**?

2. How *much* it is worth *to you?* - How do you know **how much** *value* that thing has *for you*?

We process these two parts in sequence, but we do it so fast, that it looks and feels instantaneous. We mix them into a gestalt and we are only aware of the overall experience. Let's break down that gestalt-like structure and take note of its parts, because this is where most salespersons get their hiccups. They focus on "building value", they are afraid of asking for money [in return for their offer], they are unsure if their product is worth that much, they are uncomfortable asking to get paid for doing something that's easy and pleasant for them to do (although they paradoxically believe, however, that it's ok to be highly paid for doing something they hate, and have no problem asking a lot for that!)... and I believe that these issues have root in the misunderstanding of 'what is value'.

Value Always and Only Exists in The Mind of the Evaluator/ Receiver

*"If you want to shrink something, you must
first allow it to expand.
If you want to get rid of something, you must
first allow it to flourish.
If you want to take something, you must first
allow it to be given.
This is called the subtle perception of the way
things are."*
Lao-Tzu (Tao Te Ching)

Some people find it worthwhile to live in New York City. Some people find it worthwhile to own a Hummer vehicle.

Is this true for *everybody*? Do *you* find these *valuable*? I don't find them *valuable*, for instance.

How do I know if a thing is *valuable* for me or not? Simply - I imagine how my life experience would be like, when "having" or "not having" that thing. I evoke (inside myself) the *experiences* of "having" and of "not having" it and I am paying attention to the *felt sense* that I get in each case. The *feeling* that gives me the *most pleasure* or the *least pain*, wins.

That's how we "evaluate" if something has or doesn't have *value* for us – through *comparison* of the *experiences* we would have, *with* or *without* that something. In order to *evaluate* something, to tell if something is *valuable* for us, we need to put that 'something' in a *context*, into an *experience* and compare how we *feel* in relationship with that context, when that 'something' is present and when it is not.

Note: the *context* in which we put that "something" when building our *experience* is relevant to the quality of the feeling we'll have about that "something", affecting the *value* we'll assign to it.

Think of this for a moment...

If asked, I found that pretty much everybody will say that "air is *valuable*". But, really, in this *very* moment, how much "value" do you assign to the air that you are breathing? Perhaps you haven't even paid attention to your breathing lately! We tend to take for granted what we have with abundance; we don't even consider the possibility of that thing to come to an end . But, if you put in **balance** the **real possibility** of "**not** having air to breathe" – that is, you *have an experience* of **not** *having it* - you suddenly realize that, actually, *air **is** valuable.*

People know this for a long time. There are sayings on this subject, like:

- "You never know the value of what you have until you lose it"

- "Don't take things for granted because they might not be there tomorrow"

- "People say you don't know what you've got until it's gone. Truth is, you knew what you had, you just never thought you'd lose it"

- "Appreciate what you have before it becomes what you had"

Keep this in mind, because the moment will come, at the end of your sales presentation (that is, of the *experience* you give to the prospect) when you'll need to help the prospect *become aware* of the *value* they found in what they *received* from you. And the way to do that is to have them *compare* what it would be like for them, to "have" or to "*not* have" that in their lives.

A simple way to do it is "Would you like that, **or not**?" or "What **difference** would that make for you?"

That's the purpose of a "take-away" line – to make them *aware* if there *is any* value in that offer. Some people think that this "builds" value and increases the people's desire for your offer; I don't think that offering you a giant venomous spider and then "taking away" the offer, or using "scarcity", will make you want more of that spider in your apartment!

Value doesn't exist objectively or intrinsically in a thing. It's something we *become aware of* when we evaluate and compare the *experiences of having* and *not having* that.

The experience which gives us the strongest feeling (that is, the most pleasure or the least pain) is the one valuable to us.

Tony Robbins once said: "When do people really start to live? When they face death!"

Now we know that something has *value* for us. But how much *value* it has, exactly?

Value Is Always and Only Compared with Another Value (Not with the Money)

> *"The challenge of leadership is to be strong, but not rude; be kind, but not weak; be bold, but not bully; be thoughtful, but not lazy; be humble, but not timid; be proud, but not arrogant; have humor, but without folly."*
> *Jim Rohn*

I'll talk more about the concept of "money" in the next chapter. I will only mention here that "money" is a *representation of value*, invented to facilitate the *exchange of value* (which was a bit difficult as *barter*).

Imagine you open a magazine and read that a certain house has a value of 1 million dollars. Think of this for a moment... does that house have a value of 1 million dollars to *you*?

Certainly not for me! How do I know?

First, let's assume that I established that "a house" **has** *value* for me (in other words, I'd rather have one, than not); now I have to evaluate just "**how much** *value*" it actually has for me.

How do I do that?

- Unconsciously, I **consider** the amount of **money** I am asked for it and figure out what **other things/ values** I could buy with that money (since 'money' is a *representation of value*).

- Then my mind gets busy building for me *experiences* of owning those 'other things'

- Then I make **comparisons** between the *feelings* that emerge within those *experiences* **and** the *feeling* of owning that house.

- Again, the *experience* that produces the *most pleasure* or the *least pain* wins. For me, it will *mean* that *"it has more value"* so my money will go to that.

Think of this for a moment...

Let's say I want a car – I compared the alternatives of "owning a car" and "*not* owning a car" and I concluded that I want one. So, owning a car has *value* for me. Now I need to find out *how much value* it has...

Suppose I see this car for sale for $30,000. The question that arises in my mind is "Do I want to pay this money for a car? Is owning a car worth $30,000?" So my mind quickly comes to help and gives me alternatives, like: "You could buy a $10,000 second-hand car and the rest you'll invest in your business." Then it will build *experiences* for me to *feel* how it would be like in both situations, so that I could *compare* the quality and the intensity of the feelings.

If I perceive *more pleasure* or *less pain* in the first case, then I'll go for the $30,000 car.

My mind will go through the same process, regardless of the size of my bank account or of my monthly income. Obviously, the larger my wealth, the more flexibility I have in regards to the money (even if I give the $30,000 for this car, I still have plenty of money for other things, so I don't need to "give up" too much). Since there's not too much value "given up", my decision will be less distressing and easier to make. However, the process is the same - emotionally based. As a multi-millionaire, I might decide to go for the second option, simply because "being connected with people" is a high *personal value* to me and driving a second-hand car would make me *feel* more connected with people (just as an example, that is).

The ones who still believe in The Franklin Method promote that we judge rationally and analytically when making those decisions; we are not - *all* decisions are *emotional* and you may have *more emotion* linked to a particular reason.

Besides the *amplitude* of the experience you facilitated around your offer, the difference that makes the difference is this: *against what **other value** are people comparing your offer*!?! Will that bring them *more pleasure* or *less pain* than your *offer* does?

Part of your *artistry* as a salesperson consists in giving the prospect an *as rich as possible* **array of alternatives** with which he can compare your offer. This doesn't mean you negate, hide or belittle the comparisons that might lead to a "no-buy" decision. But it *does mean* that you bring to their attention *alternatives that they didn't think of*, without "manipulating" them or "pressuring" them into buying.

It's important that you clearly convey to them that they have full liberty of choice. There is no physical or even moral pressure. Thus, they feel respected, safe and secure – enough to allow themselves to fully evaluate the "yes-buy" options you presented to them – instead of automatically rejecting them, out of fear or resentment. They can feel free to have an experience of those options, adding the *feeling* of them to the *comparison procedure*.

I want to emphasize again: this doesn't mean that the client will absolutely say "yes" and buy what you offer. However, it does mean that increases the chances for that to happen, simply because now they fully considered what it would feel like to accept your offer. They now have *a vivid experience* of your solution (that they didn't have before) to compare with other experiences that they already had.

Remember, your purpose as an Heart to Heart Selling salesperson is to have only 'win-win' deals (or 'no deal', if that's not possible).

Beauty Is In the Eye of The Beholder, and So is Value

The *existence* and the *amount* of *value* for a particular good is *subjective*. Beauty is in the eye of the beholder, and so is *value*.

Think of this for a moment...

I'm sure you've been in situations where someone tried to make you buy something (X) on the pretext that "it's cheap", "it's only $9.99" – and still you didn't feel like buying it. Why? Because you didn't find *any value* in that transaction.

You didn't compare that product against the ten bucks.

First of all, you compared it against itself: how will your life look like, with or without it? Since you didn't even have at least an *experience* of it, you couldn't find any "good feeling" to associate with the ownership of that product. Thus, your life *felt the same*, with or without it – so why should you pay 10 bucks for it? There was no relevant difference you could *feel*, so you didn't assign any *value* at all to that product. You probably thought:

- "There's nothing I can do with what this guy is offering me. It won't help me increase any value in my existence."

But, let's suppose that this product could have induced a small increase of pleasure in your life – so, you found *some* value in owning it; however, you could not justify the money.

When you considered "what other things" you could buy with the $10 and felt the feelings of owning those, every one of them made you feel better than owning the (X) product of the initial offer.

Perhaps your mind judged:

- "if I give this guy the ten bucks, I don't have enough for my lunch tomorrow" (*it's either X or the lunch*), or

- "I'd rather go to a movie with that money, I feel it's more worthwhile – because I know I'll feel good seeing that movie." (*I get more value if I buy something else*)

Money that you ask for your product is – more or less - irrelevant. People don't compare your product against *the money* you ask for it, but against *another product* that they could buy with the same money.

It's not possible to compare *value* with *money*. One can only compare *value* with another *value*.

People compare the levels of *pleasure* or *pain* that the two things would create for them.

They make their buying decisions by comparing the *value* of your product (the *value* they *receive)* with the *value* of *another product* that they would have to *give in return* (or *give up buying*, since they give you the equivalent money) – just like barter.

Note: That "another product" is, indeed, considered in relationship with the *money* you ask, as representation of *value.*

Value Can Only Be Compared with Another Value

Experience/ Exercise

Think of a friend of yours, with which you don't have a particular connection. An "acquaintance" of sorts. Find one that you know their preferences about movies: for instance, they might like adventures, action, stuff like this. Call them and invite them to this Indian movie, with a lethargic love subject, where everybody dances, cries and suffers in despair. But, it's highly emotional and a lot of people find it interesting. It's true, nothing much happens during those two-and-a-half hours, there's no real action going on, but one may learn about the depths of the human loving experience.

Tell your friend that you'd like them to join you to see this movie. Moreover, you'll pay for the tickets.

What do you think, will they come with you to watch the movie?

My experience is that they will either laugh in your face or they will try to find a plausible excuse.

What's going on there?

It doesn't make sense, from a logical and "Franklin method" perspective. You offered them "value" (because supposedly you liked that Indian movie). They didn't even need to pay money for that, since you offered to pay for the tickets. Logically, they should've said "yes".

It was *no money* involved in this equation, and yet, they refused your offer. They didn't refuse it for the "money". When they *compared* the **value** they need to **give** (e.g., their time, energy, attention) with the **value** they would **receive** (watching an Indian movie that wouldn't bring them anything of what *they* wanted), they found the *exchange* inequitable.

It was *more pain* in going to that movie, comparing with doing something else.

My point is this: "money" has little importance in a sales conversation. I know I repeat myself, but I believe this is of a great significance. Salespersons focus too much on "how much [their product] costs"; they think it costs "too much" and that's why clients don't buy; they are quick in "making deals" and "giving discounts"; they look at the economy and say "people just don't have money to buy my product".

But people always *compare values* (what they *receive* with what they should *give up*). If you want them to pay that kind of money to you, then give them more value.

Obviously, this implies that you know what is value **for them**.

Think of this for a moment...

In 1929, the Stock Market crashed. The Great Depression began and it lasted 10 long years. It was the largest financial crisis of the 20th century and deeply affected people from a financial point of view.

However, interestingly enough, in the 1920's, Hollywood/ the motion picture industry was the fifth largest industry in the nation. The major movie studios expanded mostly from about 1930, when they built large grand theaters throughout the country – because it was such a large demand. People wanted to see the movies. As a matter of fact, what's called "The Golden Age of Hollywood" is the period of time between 1930 and 1948 – paradoxically, during the Great Depression era!

It doesn't make sense when you consider this from a logical and money perspective, but it makes perfect sense if you adopt the *exchange of value* way of looking at things.

At those times, people had a hard life, their financial situation was precarious, they felt insecure, their reality narrowed to focusing on survival. I think it's fair to say that they were feeling low on themselves. They didn't have that much joy in their lives. They carried a lot of uncertainty.

Now, it's just human to want something we don't have (remember the example with 'how valuable is the air for you' – when you have it, you're ok; when it becomes scarce, that's when you'll do anything to have it). Thus, people wanted to "feel good" and have some certainty in those sad times.

That's where the movie industry kicks in. For a quarter, people could "escape", "break away" from the crushingly heavy feeling of helplessness that they were carrying around all day long. During that hour and a half, they were living in a different *reality*, where they were allowed to *feel good*. They knew that, whatever happened on that big screen, they remained *safe and secure*.

Yes, they needed the money for the food, but that's a *logical* reason. People don't make buying decisions for logical reasons, but for *emotional* reasons, remember? All decisions are emotional in nature (I know I repeat myself and I do it on purpose). *'Feeling good'* for an hour was worth more than three loaves of bread (that they could have bought with the same money), because "eating the bread" wasn't bringing *any* wanted **emotion** (of course, the speculations can step on 'feeling responsible' for their families – but that's beside the point).

On the same token, very few smokers finding themselves in a financial struggle would "give up" smoking just for financial reasons. The explanation is the same as above: they link more pleasure (and, as a result, assign more *value)* to smoking, than to saving the money (just as an example).

My point in this section is this: it's ineffective, irrelevant and it makes little sense to focus *that much* on the "money", how much it costs or if the client can afford to pay.

Instead, try to sense that people are always open to *exchange value,* IF that increases the *value* in their lives. Shift your focus to finding out what do they *value,* what makes them *feel good* and, if your product *can* bring that to them, *give* them an *experience* of it, so they will *know* for themselves. There's no need for convincing, "building value", handling objections, justifying the money – all this is of no importance to them.

People are always open to *exchange value,* IF that increases the value in their lives.

All they need to know is "will the *value* that I *receive* make me *feel better* than just holding on the *value* you ask me to *give*?"

An Abstract Model of Exchange of Value

In a schematic manner, it may look like this:

1. I am offering the value Vs (*value-sell*) and for it I am asking the amount of money M;

    a) That's the exchange of value for me, as salesperson

       i. I give Vs, the value (as I see it) of my solution to the client's problem;

       ii. I receive M, as 'potential value', for me to pay rent, buy food, etc.

2. When hearing the money figure, the client spontaneously thinks of another value Vb (*value-buy*) that they could buy with money M (but which they should give up getting, if they were to buy the value Vs that I am offering);

3. In order to evaluate how much value Vs has for them, the client imagines owning Vs (in a certain context) and feels the feeling Fs brought about by the experience of that ownership;

4. In order to evaluate how much value Vb has for them, the client imagines owning Vb (in a certain context) and feels the feeling Fb brought about by the experience of that ownership;

5. If Fs gives the client more pleasure or less pain than Fb, the client will choose to own Vs.

    a) This is the exchange of value for the client:

       i. They receive Vs, the value (as they feel it) of the solution to their problem;

ii. They give Vb, the value that they "give up buying"; this is what money M represent to them. M is a representation for Vb. As a result, they assign to Vs the quality that they feel for Vb.

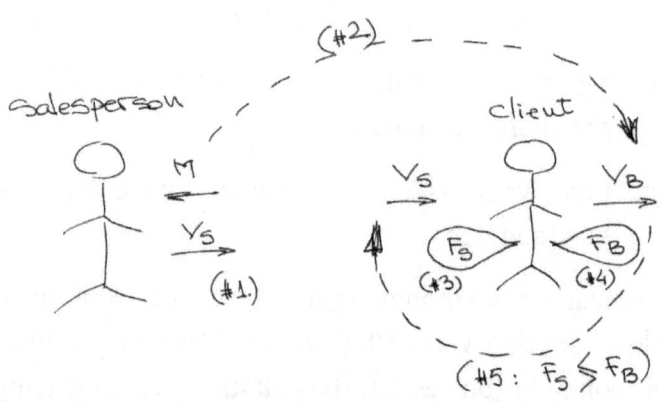

What would happen if you were to focus on your client's *reality* and get a sense of who they are, as a human being? Be genuinely curious – not just wanting to "hook" them, because they will sense (sooner or later) any tendency to manipulate them. Identify yourself with them. Be true to them. In a way, you may look at this as if you would want to "fall in love" with them, or "love" them as you love your children. Understand them, from inside-out; get a sense of where are they coming from and where do they *feel like* going.

Then, if your product happens to align with *their* desires and their ways of *being* and if it can bring them the kind of *value* they want, invite them to engage in an *experience* of what you have – don't waste your time and energy "talking" about it, trying to "convince" them and "making promises". Assure them that they will have no obligation to buy it, if they don't find value in what you have, and that you'll not pressure them in any way.

As the song says: "Give them something they can feel."

Human beings' ultimate motivation is to *feel good*. If they feel good about your offer, its *value* will increase in their mind – and, if what they need to *give* in return has a lesser *value* for them (that is, it doesn't bring them the same quality of *good feeling*), **they** will **ask** you for the *exchange*.

CHAPTER 20:

About Money

"Money is for Value what Inches are for Length."
- somebody -

People started to exchange goods among them by *barter*: the goods were exchanged directly. Although there is a debate as to why money appeared, it is commonly agreed upon the fact that *barter* exchange was rather troublesome. It required a "double coincidence of wants". In other words, both persons should've wanted what the other one had. Another hindrance for a smooth and fluent trade was raised by the indivisibility of certain goods. If I had cows and you had chickens, I would not give you an entire cow for a chicken. I would give you a leg of that cow for a chicken, but we both would need to wait until the time would come for me to kill the cow.

To make the process more fluent, **people mutually "agreed"** upon certain goods to have the role of measuring the value of all goods – today, we would call that "standard" or "currency". For instance: *salt, cattle* or *grains* where used for quantifying the value of other things. Later, *gold* was adopted as such standard, because it was easier to carry and store. Later more, that standard was symbolized merely by *paper bills*.

Note that, at the beginning, that "currency" was a *value*, in and of itself – the livestock or the grains were intrinsically useful for the people owning that, they were perceived as *valuable* and wanted by *everybody*. People could "use" them directly, they could eat the cow or plant the seeds. As a result, that "currency" was certain to constitute the subject for a further exchange.

Later, that "standard" turned a bit abstract. Gold was adopted because people mutually agreed upon it: the jewelry was attractive, making people feel good, it was also a sign of status, the material was time resistant and it was a scarce resource. Gold as currency worked as long as all people in a particular community appreciated gold as a medium of exchange and they could equate what goods they could acquire with a certain quantity of gold. Five ounces of gold, for instance, were the symbol for a certain good. Note, though, that "gold", in and of itself, has little intrinsic value: it's not much one can do with it. Its main use is to facilitate further exchanges of value.

Later on, that "currency" became entirely abstract. Paper money were printed, as a symbol of a certain quantity of gold. In other words, when we pay five dollars for a particular good, that is a symbol for the quantity of gold that was assigned as a symbol for that good (I hope it makes sense).

In other words:

Money is a symbol of a symbol.

Money symbolizes what *value* you could acquire with it, when *certain conditions* are met. The purpose of *money* is to help us quantify the *value* we intend to *exchange*.

Think of this for a moment...

Money works as a currency only to the extent that all people trust the entity who guarantees it – the bank or the government, for instance.

Somalia is evaluated as the most economically and politically unstable country in the world. What would you rather have, a hundred dollars or a million Somali Shilling?

In a sense, *money* doesn't exist. It's an *abstract* concept, just like "inches".

Money Is a Characteristic of Value

We cannot conceive "inches" on their own, but only "inches of something". The screen of my phone may measure, indeed, four inches in diagonal, but it's the screen that matters, not the inches. The inches are **only one of the characteristics** of the screen.

If someone were to tell us "For this *value* that I sell, I ask five inches", this would make no sense. We would need to know "five inches *of what?*"

The same way, when someone tells us "For this *value* that I sell, I ask five dollars", we need to figure out "five dollars *of what?*"

That "what" is the value Vb we use to compare the value Vs that's offered (see the schematic description at the end of Chapter 19).

Did you know...

People started to use the concept of "price" for a particular good only from the 13th century. The Latin "pretium" means "reward, prize, recompense".

At the very beginning of its usage, "price" was the "recompense" that the buyer would give back for the product they got from the seller – like a "thank you" gesture. Think of this "recompense" as the prize given to a tennis player for winning a competition; in that "old" perception, this "recompense" was the "price" that people paid for the opportunity to admire that player's performance.

I guess that the selling process went like this (I couldn't find any documentation, unfortunately):

- The salesperson would bring value to someone's life genuinely out of generosity and intrinsic motivation, without asking any material reward in return;

- Then, as appreciation for that value, the buyer would voluntarily give a 'price' to the salesperson.

It was only after another hundred years that it was first documented the expression "to set the price for something".

Did you know...

The Inca empire – the largest and most advanced in South America – had no concept of "money". Their "government" would give to the people all the basic necessities for living (food, housing, clothing, etc.) in return for physical labor to the state. That's how they managed to build palaces, a wide system of roads and expand their empire. There was no need for 'money' as a medium of exchange (especially as there were no stores to buy goods from!).

Learning to think in terms of *value* and *exchange of value,* instead of *money* (e.g., "how much money is something worth") will make a tremendous difference in the way you approach and handle financial transactions. (A financial transaction is an agreement carried out between a buyer and a seller to exchange an asset for payment).

Many salespersons are "afraid" of asking for money in exchange for what they sell and that happens because they focus on the *money* – "is my product too expensive?", "do they find my product too expensive?", "do they have the money?".

At some level, they feel awkward about asking for money, because they don't know if their product is 'valuable enough' for the client. And, the reason they don't know it, is because they don't focus on the value, but on the money. It's a Catch 22.

People always buy *value*. If the *value* is high enough for them, they will find the resources (the money, that is) to buy it, by giving up some other "less valuable" things for which now they are paying for. So, provide more value and money will cease to be an issue.

And, remember, they estimate the *value* by how *good they feel* about it, when they *compare* it with something else (see Chapter 19. About Value and Exchange of Value). That's probably why people don't save money for their retirement, but instead they buy a big screen TV, to watch the games. There's not that much *good feeling* about saving for retirement (at least, not *real* enough for them), but it's a *great feeling* about seeing the players real size on their wall!

Note: this is a general example. I realize that not *all* people do the same. Some people do save for their retirement and find pleasure in that.

Others buy a cruise to Alaska, instead of the TV.

CHAPTER 21:

About "Giving and Asking" and the Exchange of Value Model

"Morality, like Art, means drawing a line someplace."
Oscar Wilde

I mentioned a paradox that happens in the minds of most salespeople (business owners are also salespeople), especially if they provide some sort of service in which they are *personally* involved (therapists, coaches, physicians, etc.). They frequently feel that, if they *like and enjoy* what they do, it's *not ethical* for them to charge [that much] for their service.

From the interviews and conversations I had with people experiencing these situations, I deducted that this paradox is most probably generated by the Christian ethics about "giving". The Christian religion is all about *giving*. The Bible is so emphatic about our responsibility to *give,* but relatively silent about rules for *refusing, stop giving* or *asking.* There's no clear reference to *asking for something* in return for what you give or even about the appropriateness of *asking* in certain circumstances, as a gesture of reciprocity. This meme [unconsciously] makes many people uncomfortable when *asking* for something; unfortunately, when their frustration accumulates and bursts out, they do the *asking* in a rude and demanding manner.

However, we all generally agree that *giving* works better when *paired* with *asking* for something in return, rather than alone.

Even so much so when the *asking* it is done elegantly and naturally.

Think of this for a moment...

Parents who keep *giving* everything to their children, in any conditions and regardless of the children's attitudes will soon find that their youngsters developed a strong sense of entitlement; they demand more and more and they are never satisfied. Their sense of value distorted, because they were never *asked* for anything in return for what they received.

In other words, they could not build a *sense of value* for what they received, because they were never in a position where they could compare what they received with something else that they would give in return. Since they 'gave nothing', the estimated value of what they received was also 'nothing'.

Many relationships go astray because one of the partners is weak in enforcing their own values. Perhaps one keeps tolerating the lack of sensitivity of one's partner in the name of "*giving* unconditional love". Or perhaps one endures the offence without asking one's partner to respect one's values. Thus, that relationship becomes "abusive" – even if only at the level of thoughts and feelings.

Yes, but...

Yes, but love is something that we should do unconditionally – I can hear you saying...

I agree that **love** should be unconditionally given. Actually, the way I see it, "loving each other" is pre-programed deeply within us. I don't think we can stop loving each other, but only pretend that we do. However, **friendship**, on another hand, is something that we *do, deliberately* and *voluntarily*, that's why I consider it much more valuable. It is a *gift* – a part of ourselves that we *choose* to reveal and give to others.

In this sense, remaining in an abusive relationship (while resenting it, that is) is not about "love" anymore, but about "fear". One continues to give one's friendship to someone who doesn't respond back in an appropriate way, although this response is desired, out of fear of losing something (i.e., the security of a relationship). The abusive partner receives something without having to give anything in return; thus, they have nothing to compare the value of what they receive. The value of what they receive is compared with the value of what they give; since they gave 'nothing', the value of what they receive is also 'nothing'.

This is what we should condition and stop if our requests are not met. Why? Because there is a huge difference between "giving a gift" and "being *demanded* or *psychologically pressured* to continue gifting without any worthwhile exchange of value".

"God loves a cheerful giver" (the Bible tells us, in 2 Corinthians 9:7). When someone is *forced* to give or when someone is afraid of the consequences of 'stop giving', then they are not "cheerful" anymore. Christian generosity is about 'willingness to give', not about 'forcing the giving'.

Exchange of Value Creates Perception of Value

It seems to me that "what's received for free is not valued" or "value only received, without giving anything back, it's not truly appreciated" (generally speaking, of course, because I realize there are many exceptions).

The value of what we receive is compared with the value of what we give; when we give 'nothing', the value of what we receive is also 'nothing', for us.

We evaluate (assign value to) what we receive by comparing it with what we have to give in return.

The higher the value of what we decide to give, the higher the value we assign to what we receive.

Think of this for a moment....

Have you ever received something for free (e.g., an advice or a book) and you never used it?

Have you ever been to an "all you can eat" buffet and you ate much more than you needed to, just because you paid for the ticket, and the cost was the same, regardless of how much you would consume?

Have you ever gave something for free to someone, just to find out months later that they never made use of that?

From a Christian perspective, it's not "right" to *ask* for something you give, only because all that you have has been *given* to you (talking from a spiritual perspective, that is).

When God asks people for things (for offerings or for certain behaviors, according to the Bible), He is not asking because He *needs* something from them, but in order to *educate* them, to *teach* them a principle – just as the parents in the above example should've done. He is loving and His love is endless and, in the same time, He knows that we could receive and appreciate His love only when we *seek* for it.

On the same token, when you ask somebody for what you want, ask from the *right place*. Instead of asking from a standpoint of need or greed, ask from an attitude of facilitating for them to truly appreciate and respect the *value* of what they receive.

Ask From the Right Place

The "healthy" principle to live by is **"To engage only in *exchanges of value*, since this is the only way for the value to grow"**.

You see, your position is not anymore one of "I *need* something *from* you", but one of "I *engage only in exchanges of value*. I will give you this, but *only if you value it* – and I will know how much you *value* it by the *value* of what you are *willing to exchange*. If you don't see value in what I give, that's OK and I will not engage in this transaction – nobody loses anything. But if you do, I'll be happy to."

The metaphor that comes to mind is that of a "restriction" which it is imposed to a plant, for instance, in order for that plant to grow straight and healthy. *Restrictions* give a direction. The waterbed through which a river flows is a *restriction* and it's a good thing, because the alternative is a flood.

Thus, the *asking* is not anymore a *condition* for the thing that's *given*, but a *restriction* which causes the *receiver* to start *evaluating* that particular thing (in the Chapter 19 "About Value and

Exchange of Value" we discovered that we become aware of the *value* of something only when we compare it with "not having" it).

If we were to look at "asking for something in return" not from the perspective of a "selfish demand", but as bringing an aid for the *receiver* to truly become aware if the offering we make has *value* to them or not – then we would become free to realize that by 'asking' we make the *receiver* a service. Indeed, it may not please their Ego, but it will serve their True Self, because people put energy on the things they value.

How do you mean, **you serve people by restricting your offer?**

Let me give you an example.

Suppose I am selling pens, at five dollars each. I am making this 'offer' (the pen) to you and I present my 'restriction' for it (the five dollars).

Firstly, you can either accept the offer or reject it. You can compare the two options (of owning or not owning a pen). Thus you'll realize **if** the pen has **any** value for you at all, to start with! If it makes no difference for you, then the transaction is over. But if you realize that actually the pen *has value* for you (perhaps you feel better when you think of owning it, comparing with not, because it solves a problem for you) then your mind will go to the next step.

Secondly, you'll quickly and automatically think of what else you should "give up" buying if you were to give me the five dollars. If you perceive that 'something else' as having *more value* for you (most probably, if it makes you *feel better* when you think of that, comparing with how you feel when thinking of the pen), then you won't accept the exchange. However, if you find *less value* in that 'something else' than in owning my pen, you'll find the exchange to your advantage and you'll accept it.

Now, in your mind, my pen has the value of **that** 'something else' that you compared it with.

If the value of that 'something else' is low and trivial, then this is the value you'll assign to the pen, too. That's why, generally, for a billionaire, the pen will have little value. Also, that's why getting something for free has *little* to *no value* to someone.

However, if the value of that 'something else' is high and of a significant *importance* to you, then you'll appreciate my pen on the same scale. That's why the more you pay for something, the more you appreciate it, cherish it and put *effort* to make good use of it.

What I am *asking* (the *restriction* I set) for my pen is a tool for **you** to become *aware*: (#1) of the *existence of value* and (#2) of the *amount* that this *value* has for **you** – as long as I am not forcing you (by any means) to accept it! My inner attitude should be one of *presence, innocence* and *equanimity* in regards to your answer.

Think of this for a moment...

There is another interesting phenomenon that comes to life when asking for something in return for what we give.

This works the same as the for the beliefs we entertain. Remember the Ouroboros motif symbolizing the serpent eating its own tail, suggesting something that keeps re-creating itself (see Chapter 8). Or the 'commitment and consistency' principle (Cialdini). Or the concept of a 'hypnotic loop'. Or the "Cobb loop", from the movie "Inception", noting that we are *creating* and *perceiving* our reality in the same time. James Tripp wrote somewhere "As human beings, we co-create our reality. What we experience as everyday reality is not really reality at all – it is just the *sense* we make of reality rather than reality itself."

The "reality" of the value we perceive in something works the same way:

1. I like this house (that is, I have a strong pleasant feeling about it), so I decided to wholeheartedly pay 1 million dollars for it (and I feel the same strong pleasant feeling about that).

   a) Having ownership for the decision is of the essence.

   b) The slightest sense that I've been manipulated or forced in taking this decision will break this cycle.

2. Since I paid 1 million dollars (and I feel good about that), this means that I should feel the same about the house (reinforcing my initial perception of its great value)

   a) Then the cycle restarts from #1.

My decision to assign a certain value to a thing will reinforce in my mind and (paradoxically) *will become the reason* for believing that the thing really has that value. When I feel it as valuable and I have an experience of that feeling, it becomes my new reality.

The main theme is that *value only given* or *only taken* is of little use. Only *exchange of value* is conducive to the *increase of value*. However, there is a difference between thinking and saying "I can give you this, but you **must** give me that, I *demand* that in return" and the attitude of "I *engage only in **exchanges** of value*. I will give you this *only if you value it* – and I will know how much you *value* it by the *value* of what you are *willing to exchange*."

That gives you the permission to stop worrying about *asking* for value when *offering* something of value. As long as you keep a *candid attitude*, both of you will become *aware* and realize **if** that 'something' has **any value at all** and **how much value** it has. It will highly serve both of you, you'll appreciate it properly and it will bring you more satisfaction.

It will make you *feel good.*

CHAPTER 22:

About Handling Objections

"Act without doing; work without effort."
Lao-Tzu (Tao Te Ching)

If the prospect brings up any objections following the *experience* of my *solution* and my *asking* for *exchange,* it means either that the *experience* I gave was weak and they could not extract *value* from it or it was *irrelevant* to them (there was really no value in my solution, for them).

In the Chapter 26 "H2H Selling major guidelines" I will explain in detail why the prospect might raise objections, dismissing your offer for exchange, and what "possible directions" you have from there.

However, **the proper moment to address those objections is BEFORE they even show up.**

Objections are different from "asking clarifying questions" – those are welcomed and I'll answer those the best I can, at the proper moment.

I invite you to consider those "possible directions" that I mentioned above (and described on Chapter 26, at the "If they Refuse my offer" Subchapter), and incorporate those **inside** and **during** the *experience* you give them.

For instance:

- Do your best to *be present and connected* while giving your prospect the experience of your solution; make this your priority, rather than 'building value' or 'making them buy';

- Do your best to *engage their attention* while giving them that experience;

- Ask them 'feed-back' questions, to confirm that what you show them is still of interest for them, that they are still *engaged* with you and that they consider how it may be of value for them (in other words, facilitate for them to actually have an experience);

- If they feel value in your solution, assist them to quantify that value by suggesting comparisons with other things that they are familiar with, so to prime their mind: "I'm curious, just to get a sense if there's a good fit for what we do here: if you were to have this [the solution you propose], and as you consider the value that this has for you, what else in your life has a similar value?"

  - You could, perhaps, even be specific: "would that be the same valuable to you as a flat screen TV?" (this is just an example).

The *principle* to keep in mind is this: in order for them to say *no* to my offer, most probably:

- they *focus* on something (which prevents them from recognizing *value* in my offer), and/ or

- they do *not focus* on something else (which, if they did, they would say *yes*).

So, bring to their awareness the things they *are not focusing on*, and put the things they *are focusing on* into a larger and richer perspective.

Experience/ Exercise

Find a partner. Imagine I just gave you $100. You need to share some of that money with your partner (50-50, 80-20, whatever you like). Make your offer to your partner.

Here's the trick: if they accept the offer you make, you both keep the money. If they don't, neither of you gets it. In other words, you *both* get some money or *neither* of you do.

If they say *no*, this shows that perhaps they *focus* on what *you get* and *not focus* on what *they get* and that they will get *nothing* if they don't agree.

Repeat this exercise with different partners. With some, wait until they say *no* and try to "handle their objection". With others, *prime* their mind by presenting these *focusing* perspectives from the very beginning, when you describe the game.

Notice which ones are more prone to say *yes* to your offer.

"Handling objections" *after* they have been voiced-up is a challenge: frustrating for the salesperson and annoying for the prospect.

Think of this for a moment...

How would *you* like to have *your* objections "handled" when discussing an issue with your boss?

Not a happy perspective, is it?

To bring "arguments" in order to "handle objections"

presupposes that *decisions* are made logically – only that they are not! All decisions are emotional, so logical arguments have little relevance. And, the moment for activating *[the decision making] emotions* is **during** the *experience* you give them – not after the prospect activated their *[objection raising] emotions*.

"Yes, but..."

Some "heavy-duty" salespersons argued that they could bring up arguments to *make* the prospect change their mind. It's true, I did that, I know it can happen. But, some of those clients cancelled the agreement the next day; some resented the transaction and they wasted much of my time with their complaints; some didn't even use the service I "convinced" them to buy or, if they did, they did it in derision and, obviously, it didn't work.

Tad James says: "You don't need clients. You want clients who get results."

It's useful to be aware that "decision" only refers to a particular moment of the process of "deciding" – and that process never ends. The client may take *now* the decision that you push them to make, but *later* they will make another decision, the one that *they* want, to *their* benefit - since you, as a salesperson, you are not anymore around to pressure them into making the decision of buying, *against* their benefit.

Remember, "A man convinced against his will is of the same opinion still".

CHAPTER 23:

About Intention vs Expectation, or Want vs Need

"Therefore, without being attached to the fruits of activities, one should act as a matter of duty; for by working without attachment, one attains the Supreme. "
Bhagavad-Gita

I pointed out a few times that you, as a salesperson, have to maintain your equanimity, your serenity, innocence and *noble indifference* about the prospect's response to your offer or about the results of your actions. That is, you better forget about your *needs* when entering that interaction.

This does *not* mean that you don't *want* for the transaction to happen. However – since your principle of life is to **engage only in exchanges of value** – that means that *you* **accept** the transaction **only** if the prospect (#1) perceives *value* in your offer and (#2) they *wholeheartedly accept the restriction* you are *asking* for (which shows you that they assign proper *value* to your offer, leading to greater chances that they will make good use of it).

That means that you don't **need** for that transaction to take place under **any** conditions. A *needy* attitude like that would make *you* "needy"; not only this is unattractive and shows lack of self-respect (which will evoke the client's disrespect, as well), but it will also *devalue* your offer and it will make the transaction less probable.

When the thing you are offering is perceived as having low value (which happens when you're acting "needy"), you are not truly serving your clients. Even if they buy your product, they will put little value on it, they will not appreciate it properly and they will make little use of it. They might even not use it at all, considering it a waste of time.

When you're "needy", you basically make the selling process *about you* and *your needs*, having little to no considerations for *their needs* and *wants*.

Yes, *be clear* about your *intention*: you want to *sell/ offer* your product to as many people as possible, and have *clients* who find *value* in it! However, your *attitude* is not anymore "how can I *make* people buy my stuff", but:

- How can I *connect* with people?

- How can I inspire them to *be present* during the *experience* I am *giving* them for my *solution*, so that they truly see it for what it is *now* for them, without bringing pre-judgments from their past?

- How can I give them a *powerful experience* of my solution, so that they *feel the value* of it?

- How can I assist them with the *evaluation* process, so that they become clear if my *solution* is *valuable* for them or not?

- How can I support them in this process, so that they consider comparing my *offer* with various *values* from their life, in order to make a *more complete* image of it?"

After you became clear about this *intention* and you feel it as real, forget about it, forget about *you* and *your wants* (or, rather, put all that on the back of your mind).

Some trainers suggest that the salesperson should sustain *the expectation* that the prospect will buy. Personally, I don't find that all so useful, because all that hope and anticipation will also bring about the fear of 'not happening', which will only make you more attached to the outcome. Expectation implies "prediction", "promise", which tends to induce passivity and 'waiting for it to happen'.

Other trainers suggest the old "keep your eyes on the prize"; but if you do that during the interaction with your prospect, then you'll make that interaction 'about *you*' and 'what *you* want', rather than 'about *them*' and 'the value *they* receive'.

I believe that the real scope of the advices above is to help you keep your mind on what you *want*, rather than on what you *don't want* or to prevent your mind to go on the "negative expectations". I agree and align with that: build a strong positive image of the world the way you want to create it; build a strong and rich mental representation of the successful resolution of your sales interaction. Allow the feeling of that representation to emerge and *immerse* in it. Allow its vibration to touch every molecule of your body. Let *this feeling* to be your Intention.

Then, let go of it. Become present to the moment. Put your conscious mind and your Ego aside and allow your unconscious mind to take care of the unfolding of the events, based on the feeling you "set" as a target.

When you are talking with a prospect, focus entirely on *them* and *their* wants and needs. Everything else is gone, vanished, empty. Connect with them and *serve* them just as if you loved them deeply, just as if they were your loved brother or sister. That's what our profession is about, actually!

Steve Chandler and Rich Litvin put it clearly in their book, The Prosperous Coach: "It's either a Hell Yeah! for both of us or it's a Clear No!"

CHAPTER 24:

About Enthusiasm

"Nothing great was ever achieved without enthusiasm."
Ralph Waldo Emerson

Enthusiasm means different things to different people. Most probably, when someone tells you to "be more enthusiastic" or "show some enthusiasm", they want you to show excitement, be loud, move your hands, be bold, lively and overly energetic, etc.

This is just another example of a semantic shift that concepts take over time.

Etymology shows us that the source of this word comes from the Greek 'enthousiasmos', whose root is 'entheos'; this is a compound word, formed from "en" (meaning "in", "within") and "theos" (meaning "god").

Thus, we reach the original meaning of the word, which is "having the god within". Better yet, we should say "becoming *connected* with the god within", since "god" it is already in all of us.

That's exactly what happens when we allow ourselves to *become present to the moment of now* – we *connect* with *what is*, with ourselves and with our environment (if there was any difference...) and feel the *joy of life* created moment by moment, so we can look at it as if it is for the first time we see it. This is what really means to "be alive" – to *feel life*, as it happens *right now* (see Chapter 17 "About Presence").

When you *become present*, full of *joy* and *compassion*, looking at the world as if through the eyes of a child, with amusement and curiosity, free of the Ego's stories about who you are, what you should do or how the world is – that's when you have **enthusiasm!**

CHAPTER 25:

About Play

What I'm talkin' about is a game... A game that can't be won, only played... […] Yeah the rhythm of the game, just like the rhythm of life...

[…] Put your eyes on Bobby Jones... Look at his practice swing, almost like he's searchin' for something... Then he finds it... Watch how he settle himself right into the middle of it, feel that focus... He got a lot of shots he could choose from... Duffs and tops and skulls, there's only ONE shot that's in perfect harmony with the field... One shot that's his, authentic shot, and that shot is gonna choose him... There's a perfect shot out there tryin' to find each and every one of us... All we got to do is get ourselves out of its way, to let it choose us... Can't see that flag as some dragon you got to slay... You got to look with soft eyes... See the place where the tides and the seasons and the turnin' of the Earth, all come together... where everything that is, becomes one... You got to seek that place with your soul Junuh... Seek it with your hands don't think about it... Feel it... Your hands is wiser than your head ever gonna

*be... Now I can't take you there Junuh... Just
hopes I can help you find a way... Just you...
that ball... that flag... and all you are...
Bagger Vance, "The Legend of Bagger Vance"*

The closest idea that I found to nicely match this Heart to Heart Selling theory is the concept of *play*. The best attitude or frame of mind to have while *selling* Heart to Heart is one of *playfulness*.

As we grow into adulthood and take in all sorts of cultural "commands", we become "machines" running for achieving an end-result, which, we hope, will bring us what we really want – happiness, fulfillment, satisfaction. And we were led to believe that we need to *work hard* and to achieve many material things before we are allowed to feel that.

Everything we do became a means to an end. We do something "in order to" *get* something else. When we talk to prospects while carrying this attitude, it turns *selling* into a process "about *us* and what *we* want", instead of "about *them* and what *they* want".

Think of this for a moment...

I know you had that weird experience, when you believed that getting something (a sum of money, a car, a house, whatever) will make you happy. And, indeed, you've been happy and euphoric for a couple of weeks, perhaps a month; then you became unsatisfied again and your mind set you up for yet another goal to accomplish so you can be happy.

And, in doing so, we miss the point. That feeling we are looking for is *already inside* of us, only that it's carefully hidden by our Ego, with intricate stories about what we need to do first.

The Attitude of Play

Look at the children - they are happy while *playing with no end in mind,* for no purpose. As a matter of fact, the moment you make the game about winning, they lose interest quickly. Why? Because you just turned their *play* into *work,* implying that they can enjoy themselves only if they reached a certain result. This instills *fear* - the fear of not achieving *that end result. Fear* kills *play.* One needs to feel *safe and secure* in order to *play.*

When the purpose of the activity becomes more important than the activity itself, then it's not *play* anymore.

It becomes *work.* From this perspective, we can see *work* as an activity that is very much *outcome oriented.* This is not inherently bad or evil. However, more often than not, this attitude slides into running after a *toxic outcome* and we become *fearful* and *needy,* because we end up linking our sense of self-worth with the achievement of that outcome. And we know that this is true when we start feeling bad about ourselves, angry or frustrated, if things don't work out the way we meant.

This is why the real opposite of *play* is not really *work,* but *depression.* When we take those inherent failures personally, to the heart, we start to feel hopeless, worthless and helpless.

Experience/ Exercise

If you find yourself dreading the possibility that the prospect might say *no* to you, then you are not in the *play* state anymore. You just became *needy.*

Take a deep breath, mentally step back, become aware that you are thinking "needy" thoughts and distance yourself from them –

look *at them* with *"cold and empty eyes"*... emotionless eyes. Relax around your eyelids and *center* yourself. Breathe deeply, feel that air and feel your body from within. Feel your legs. Feel the *space* around your head, neck, shoulders and all around your body. Experience yourself as if you were "suspended" and "floating" in the air. *Expand your awareness.* Enjoy a *relaxed focus* and allow every breath you take to *relax* you even more.

Now allow the object of your need to pass, let go of it and resume talking with your prospect.

Note: when I say "feel [something]" (your breathing, your skin, etc.), I don't mean to actively "**do** the feeling". "Doing/ Thinking" are attributes of your Ego. "Feeling" is an attribute of your True Self. Fact is that you are "feeling" those sensations anyway, all the time; you are not paying attention to them, though. So, all you need to do is "stop the doing", slow down and just *pay attention; allow* that "feeling" some room in your *awareness.* There's *no effort, no forcing* that you need to make.

Play is enjoyable in and of itself. It's done for its own sake. *Play* is our natural state we were created to be in, when we don't get in our way. There is no "burnout", no "frustration" or "feel bad about self" when one is engaged in a state of *playing. Play* engages our *creativity,* our sense of *freedom* and *connection* with others. "If you want to belong, you need social play", says Dr. Stuart Brown, a pioneer in the research of *play.*

Thus, *play* could be an elegant answer to the 'fear of rejection' phenomenon.

Play helps us learn social skills. Play stimulates neural growth in amygdala, the center of our emotions. It also contributes to the

178

development of the pre-frontal cortex, the place where we make decisions. In other words, *play* helps us become more emotionally mature and better decision makers. If you think about it, pretty much all the essential things you know today, you learned them through *implicit learning* – playing the game, rather than learning the rules of the game first.

Playful vs Childish

Some people argue that *playing* means *not responsible,* frivolous, superficial. This is a huge misunderstanding of what *play* really is. A tennis player winning the Wimbledon tour is anything BUT superficial or 'not responsible'; she is *highly engaged* in what she is doing. However, in the same time, she is having fun, she loves what she is doing; she is *in the flow*. In that moment, the game itself is more important than winning.

An artist experiences the same state – be it an actor on stage, a singer during a concert or a painter in his studio. That *play state* is an act of *creativity*, of deep *connection* with what they do and with their environment (people and things around them). The end result of that activity – although set as an *intention* – is now out of their preoccupations. They are totally immersed in the activity.

Think of this for a moment....

Most people have a hobby, something they like to do for the sheer pleasure of doing it. Yes, they have a certain *intention* for an end result they would like to reach, but that is *only secondary.* Even if they don't achieve that, they are still happy and ready to try it again, later.

Do you think that this sort of attitude would help a salesperson in their activity?

If you were to adopt this resourceful perspective when *selling*, how would that be helpful to *you*?

The *state* that the salesperson has when entering a *sales conversation* is essential. Have you ever been in a situation where a prospect refused your offer and you became so frustrated and angry, that you messed-up the next appointment, too? When you are frustrated, your mind is in your *past* (running over the events that caused that frustration). When your mind is *not in the present moment*, your prospect's mind will *not be in the present moment*, neither. That means they are not even listening to you. They are not paying attention to you. You are two separate entities who give no attention to the other, but only to their own thoughts.

When you cannot *connect* with your prospect, they will not be *present with you* and they will not see *value* in what you show them. Thus, they will not buy it.

It will be a waste of time.

Think of this for a moment....

I'm sure you heard in your sales trainings about the *metaphor* of "kids are the best salespersons on the planet". The argument is that they have no inhibitions: if they want something, they ask for it; if they get a *no*, they ask again and again, until they get it.

The distinction that those trainers fail to make is that children are *present in the moment* when they do all those commendable things. They have no fear, because there is nothing to fear in the *present* – fear is always in the *future*. They ask for what they want, because they are not running in their minds any stories about why they shouldn't do it or about what others will think about them if they do. They ask again and again - but each time they ask it's **as if it is for the first time;** they carry no grudge from the previous refusals (because when they do and they start a tantrum, they are not fun anymore, are they?). If they are told *no*, they innocently ask "Why?" – but not with a spirit of interrogation or with a clear ulterior motive of cleverly destroying your reasons. Not at all. They ask out of *genuine curiosity*, and *that's* what makes them so disarming.

You'll be capable to do all that when you are in a state of *playfulness* and *presence.*

Note – I always had troubles agreeing with this metaphor before realizing the distinction above, because children are generally accepted anyway, in whatever they do (e.g., even if they poop or fart, people would find that funny, somehow!). That's why I want to make a clear differentiation between Being Playful and Being Childish.

- Being Childish is immature, silly and frivolous. There is no respect, consideration or awareness of other people's feelings. You know that people will consider offensive what you're about to do, but you're doing it anyway, as if in contempt or unkindness.

- Being Playful is a state of *presence*, and this requires *awareness* and *alertness*. Whatever you do, it starts from an honest innocence.

Experience/ Exercise

What if you were to do this next little exercise **before** a sales presentation? (you could rehearse it at home, so it becomes a second nature for you; that will shorten your preparation time before the appointment).

Stop for a moment, *connect with yourself* and *become present*. You can use some of the recordings on the http://www.hearttoheartselling.com/mindfulness.html, or simply sit down, close your eyes and pay attention to your breathing. Allow your awareness to expand, to "catch" sounds in your environment or sensations on your body, for instance. Allow a sense of awareness for the space around your body to slowly and gradually increase, all by itself, while you are only paying attention to what happens now.

As you do this, go back and remember a time when you felt *playful, joyful* and *free*. Remember that time, as vividly as you can – where were you, with whom, what was happening, how were you feeling... Be like a movie director who wants to re-create that scene and needs as many details as possible. Look at that scene through your own eyes, as if you *are* there, *now*. Feel those feelings *now*. Don't force them, just *evoke* them and allow them to arise naturally. Then, enjoy them. Pay attention and become aware of what's different now for you, comparing with couple of minutes ago. What do you notice that's different, now that you have those playful feelings?

Now, take this state, those feelings of *playfulness* and *imagine* that you just ended the sales presentation (that you're about to enter) and the prospect joyfully accepted your offer. Put that image in the midst of these *playful* feelings you feel now. Perhaps you can feel your client feeling *playful*, as well.

Now, go back a couple of minutes inside the sales presentation, carrying the same feelings of *playfulness* – in you and in your client. Imagine you are almost finishing your presentation (the experience you gave to your client) and he is entirely captivated by that experience.

Go back a few more minutes, to a time where you are talking about a particular section of your presentation. Imagine both of you feeling *connected* and *playful*, entirely at ease, as if you were old friends. He is asking questions, you answer them and he is pleased with the *value* he feels in what you show him.

When that *reality* is vivid enough in your system, open your eyes, *remain present* and in hold on to that *playful* state. Put aside any *intention* that you have for the outcome of the appointment. Stop thinking about what *you* want. Trust that your unconscious mind will guide your words and behavior, according to that "forgotten" Intention. Just enjoy the *presence*, the *connection* with yourself and with your environment.

Now you're ready to meet your prospect. Go ahead and have fun.

CHAPTER 26:

H2H Selling Major Guidelines

"I think we have to change metaphors. We have to go from what is essentially an industrial model of education, a manufacturing model, which is based on linearity and conformity and batching people. We have to move to a model that is based more on principles of agriculture. We have to recognize that human flourishing is not a mechanical process; it's an organic process. And you cannot predict the outcome of human development. All you can do, like a farmer, is create the conditions under which they will begin to flourish."
Sir Ken Robinson, on his TED talk "Bring on the learning revolution!"

The message of this quote fits perfectly with the message I want to convey in this book.

The current paradigm of selling is built on top of an "industrial" model. The industrial age mindset is one of control and linearity: "if you do *this*, it will happen *that*". Most sales trainings promise you that you will be able to "make people buy" – everybody and in any conditions - if you just "apply" their techniques. They consider people (i.e., the clients) as machines, and if you, the salesperson, push the right buttons, they will buy whatever from you. They make you believe that it's just that simple and it's *your fault* if people don't buy. Sales managers believe that, too, so they pressure their team to go out and try harder, push for the sale, "make them" buy. Marketing guru's heavily use words like "leads generation", "funnel" or "silver bullet".

Most salespersons become frustrated and feel bad about themselves exactly because they start from the expectation that if they just "do the steps", people *will automatically* buy from them.

It's not like that. Life is not linear, nor mechanical – it's organic, it's complex. Heisenberg, generally regarded as the father of quantum mechanics, said: "Not only is the Universe stranger than we think, it is stranger than we **can** think."

Yes, people behave in patterns and things can be influenced, but life, people and events are too complex to be controlled. Influence is not a linear process... You may influence people by *setting up the conditions* that offer the *best probability* for them taking a certain direction. However, there are NO guarantees in life and acting from a stance of expecting them to exist will only set you for frustration and disappointment.

However, although you can't control *everything*, there are things you *can* control. Stephen Convey said in his "Seven Habits of Highly Effective People": "We are not in control; Principles control. We control our actions, but the consequences that flow from these actions are controlled by Principles."

When you start to consider *influencing life*, in general – and the *selling* activity, in particular – from this perspective, you can become free of the pressure of "getting" a *certain* result. "Letting go of the need" for that "certain result" makes sense now, because you realize that all you can do is to set up proper conditions, while knowing and accepting that it's *impossible* to predict the actual outcome. That outcome it is only a *probability*, never a *certainty*. Stop judging yourself by the results you have; rather, focus on *setting the proper context*, making sure you respect your *personal values* and the *principles of life.*

Think of this for a moment...

No matter how hard you try, you'll not be able to fly by jumping up, because the *principle of gravity* will pull you down. This will continue to happen as long as you ignore the *principles*. However, when you consider the other *principles* (the density of air, velocity, etc.) you could set up *conditions* for flying to happen. You could build some wings, for instance.

Prepare the Conditions

In my work as a hypnotist and change-worker I learned that the most important part of my job takes place *before* the client even comes to my office. That part consisted in setting up the *conditions* for employing the *principles* that would make the desired outcome *most probable* to happen.

I learned that my *state of presence* is of the essence.

I learned that *change* happens only if I *connect* with my client.

I learned to *let go of the need* for a particular result and that I should not want it more than the client does.

I learned that if I *force* the result to happen, it won't; and to the extent that I let go of the need and I only *participate in the unfolding* of it - while allowing the principles to do the work, then it will.

I learned that the client will not "buy into" the change they claim to desire if they don't see *value* in it or if they perceive what they need to "give in exchange" as more *valuable* to them.

I learned that their engagement and willingness to have an *experience of the change that they wanted to achieve* was the main ingredient which made the difference between success and failure.

I learned that when we are *present* together (that is, we have a common object of focus and include each other in our awareness) that allows for a deep *connection* to quietly develop in both of us, which lasts for a long, long time.

Life and Selling Are Like Dancing

Life and *selling* are like *dancing* – you *connect*, you *invite* and they *choose to engage* with it; then you *lead elegantly* by "opening possibilities of movement" and *they follow*. You "create a vacuum" and *they choose* to go there, to fill it with their body. If they don't want to go there, you don't force them, because the activity will cease to be 'dance' and becomes something else ('forcing'). *Dance* only happens when there is *freedom of movement* inside this dynamic. There is no 'need' for a particular thing to happen. Anything that happens is included and accepted as part of the dance. When you don't see it this way, you'll consider any unexpected little motion as "failure", causing you frustration. But if you were to see the process like a genuine dance, then all those unforeseen events will only offer new possibilities of movement and unfolding.

Sell by "opening possibilities", by "creating a vacuum", not by "pushing".

This is Leadership.

That being said, what are the *elements* to be taken care of, the major *guidelines* or *phases* to consider, in order to open up the possibilities for successful "Heart to Heart Selling"?

Keep in mind, these are **not** "steps" to follow in a linear manner. They *may* go linearly, but I invite you to look at them as little "loops" that unfold and mix in an organic way. One loop doesn't end when you start the other; rather, they interweave together harmoniously, one blending into another. These key elements are constantly happening.

That's why the best way to understand and use these guidelines is to master them and then forget about them, allowing your unconscious mind to *indirectly* guide your thoughts, feelings and actions.

Heart to Heart Selling is not something that you *do*, but something that you *are* - something you *become* or something you *create* yourself to *be*.

Personal Preparation

- I am *present and mindful, aware* and *alert*. My *attention* is on *connecting* with people. My attitude is directed on "what can I *give TO* and *FOR* them" (not on "what can I get *FROM* them").

    ○ Some sales trainings recommend that I should "pump

up" and "energize". Instead, I found that *slowing down* and evoking a state of *presence* will make wonders, not only in opening a *connection* with the prospect, but also opening up my *creativity*, my box of *resources* and even my sense of humor. I become more relaxed; there is no auto-imposed need for me to behave in any particular way or to appear to be something else than what I am.

- After I become *present, slowed down* and *connected*, I set an *intention* for what I would like to have happen. That is, I *evoke* (I allow to emerge, not 'force') the *feeling* of that – "how would that feel, if I had it now?" I enjoy that feeling for a while, then I "forget" about it, trusting that my mind it will indirectly guide my actions towards it.

- I make a commitment to engage *ONLY* in *exchanges of value* (as opposed to just *taking* or *giving* it), because I know that *value* grows only when it is exchanged.

- I know that by formulating a *restriction* for the *value* that I give, I actually *serve* the *receiver*, because I *create the conditions* for them to truly evaluate *if* what I give has any value for them and *how much* value it has for them. That's how we will *both* know in our hearts if that interaction has any potential for an *exchange of value* in it. Also – if the prospect decides to buy – this will increase the chances that they will actually value and make good use of that purchase.

Offer a Connection

- I know that selling is about *offering a solution to a problem* that people experience – this implies that a *problem* exists and it is agreed upon; the prospect wants to experience something different in their lives and they want that *now*.

- I also know that the only reason people buy something is to *improve* their life experience and the *value* they have in their lives.

  - Thus, when I connect with people, my focus is on *discovering, acknowledging* and *addressing* that *problem* – instead of abruptly imposing my *solution*, without a *problem* to address.

  - If I need to make the conversation short, I may direct my questions towards bringing their awareness over the possible *problem* that they might have (and to which I have the *solution*, that is).

- Just as I don't dash in or burst into a temple simply because I wanted to make some offerings to the gods today, I don't importune people to listen to me, neither. Instead, I *ask for their permission* to talk to them.

  - My purpose is to *connect* with them and – possibly – to *offer* them something, not to "make them buy". Thus, I have no shadow of reluctance in initiating the conversation, because I know I don't intend to impose anything on them. I also know that I cannot impose that 'connection' on them, but I can only 'offer' it or 'facilitate' it to happen, and it's for them to accept it or not. I am 'opening the door', inviting and allowing them to enter (rather than forcing them, that is).

- My intention is to *give* them something, if it so happens that they experience a problem to which I have a solution. Thus, my attitude in initiating a conversation is the same as if they dropped a hundred dollars bill on the floor and I want to make them aware of that, so they can get it back.

- I know I need their *attention*, their *trust* and I need them to feel *safe and secure* with me.

- If they say *no*, that's fine, because it shows me that none of the conditions above would've been met.

- If they say *yes*, I can continue, aligning the *offering* with what *they* want, because I have the common sense to realize that they are interested in what *they* want, not in what *I* want.

- My *attitude* in a temple is one of humbleness, politeness and with the intention to be of service. There's no place for Ego's in a temple.

  - The same, in my conversation with somebody, my intention is to *be of service.*

  - I know that a *service* (or an *advice*, for that matter) is best received when it is *asked for.* So, I let go of any *need* of *imposing* my offer on them.

Offer an Experience of Your Solution

- If – and *only* IF – they *openly recognize* that they *have a problem* (that is, there is some *change* they want to make in their lives), then ...

   ○ I get curious, I ask questions and I go deeper to *understand how* is that a problem *to them*, what does it *mean* for them to continue to carry this problem and what it would *mean* for them to *solve* it, because I know that all decisions are *emotional* in nature.

- If – and *only* IF – they *openly recognize* that they *want a solution* AND they want it *now* (as opposed to 'next year', that is), then ...

   ○ I *offer* them an *experience* of the *solution* I have, for *them* to directly know for themselves if my *solution* is *valuable* for them, or not.

   ○ I emphasize and make sure they know that there are *no obligations* for them to buy, whatsoever, following that *experience*. I want them to feel *safe and secure* in my presence – this is what a 'relationship' is about, after all.

   ○ I point out that *my purpose* as a *salesperson* is *not* to "get people buy my product", but literally to *make the offer for an exchange of value*, while entirely respecting their decision to accept it or not. And, I really mean that!

Give Them a Real Experience that They Can Feel

When I give them that *experience of my solution*, I do it wholeheartedly, I am not holding anything back, knowing that this is the only way for them to feel the real *value* of my *offer*.

- My only focus is to maintain a *connection* between me and the prospect, by doing my best to ensure that both of us are *present to the moment*. This is the only way to facilitate for them to actually engage, be aware, see what I am showing and hear what I am saying (rather than them seeing and hearing what their *past* experiences bring to their attention). Only *this* will make that *experience* memorable and powerful to them – and this is of the essence.

- The purpose of this *experience* is to give them a real *sample* of my *solution* and for them to "feel" the *value* of it. However, I know that they need to *trust* that I will continue to deliver *exactly* what I am showing them now. Trust is vital for the existence of any *agreement*. That's why I let go of any need for them to say *yes*, and I hold my *intention* (for them to say *yes*) only on the back of my mind. I remain *present, alert* and *detached,* openly conveying to them that there is no pressure.

  - It is exactly this "no pressure" that allows the relationship to naturally develop and for them to feel *safe, secure* and *comfortable* in my presence. This increases one hundred times the chances for them to want to connect and to work with me.

- I realize that people don't buy 'things', not even 'benefits', but rather what 'those benefits' **mean** to them and the **feeling** they hold about that 'meaning'. In other words, if all they see is the 'thing', they will find *little* to *no value* in it – they might not even consider buying it. Thus, I am careful to lead their attention towards the *meaning* that the 'thing' has for them. I ask questions and I want them to answer (if they don't, that means they are not engaged in the process and that means there's no *experience* there, it's only me talking to "a wall". See Chapter 17 "About Presence").

- I realize that the *value* of a particular thing (and the meaning of it, see above) *always* lies in the eyes of the beholder.

- I realize that people become aware of the *value* that a particular thing carries for them when they start contemplating how their life experience will be like **with** and **without** that thing. Thus, I ask questions about the differences that this *solution* would make for them, if they were to have it. I will also ask questions about how would they handle the situation without my *solution*, and I want to know what would be different for them in those two scenarios (with or without my *solution*, that is).

Make an Offer for an Exchange of Value

- Supposing that the *experience* they had was great and they *feel value* in my *solution* (I might even ask them, "Do you see *value* in this, or not?", "What difference would this make for you?", etc.), then I ask for their permission to make an *offer for an exchange of value*.

- I also realize that people estimate the *value* that a thing has for them by comparing that thing with something else in their lives and noticing how each one makes them *feel*. The *money* that I ask for *my product* has little to no relevance; people will consider 'what other *value*' they could buy with the same amount of money and then they will compare how they *feel* in regards to those two alternatives (see Chapter 19 "About Value and Exchange

195

of Value").

- Remember the schematic diagram at the end of Chapter 19:

  - I offer the value Vs (*value-sell*) and ask the money M;

  - The client "transforms" the money M into another value Vb (*value-buy*), that they could buy with this money, but which they should "give up" getting, if they were to choose to own the value Vs that I am offering;

  - Then the client *evaluates* the "size" of each value (Vs and Vb) by imagining themselves owning each one of the *values* and noting how each experience makes them *feel*; they consider the feelings Fs and Fb;

  - Then the client compares those values (Vs and Vb) by comparing the feelings (Fs and Fb); the feeling which will bring them more pleasure or less pain will indicate the higher value, that they will end up choosing.

- I know that when people say *no* to an offer, they – most probably:

  - Focus on something, and/ or

  - Not focus on something else (which, if they did, they would say *yes*).

- So, I want to:

  - Bring to their awareness the things that they are

not focusing on, and

- Put the things they are focusing on into a larger perspective.

o That's why when I introduce the *money* figure, I may also suggest some comparisons that I want existent in their mind – along *with* their own. I might contrast the possibility and the *pleasure* of solving their problem (with all the *meanings* associated with that) against something carrying less meaning in their life and the *pain* (or *less pleasure*) produced by that – but for which they paid or *are paying* the same amount of money.

o Note – somebody pointed to me that this is "manipulation" and I don't think it is. Why? Because I don't intend to make them feel guilty or ashamed (in order to manipulate them to buy, that is) and I don't stop them from making their own comparisons. I only bring to their attention this particular *factual*, however *distressing* situation – where they spent money on something that was worthless. I am only opening the window toward this comparison, too, so that they would consider it – because it is real and true. I am not closing down their option to compare my product with something else, that might lean them towards "not buying". I am only directing their attention to things that they might tend to be oblivious to or embarrassed to look at.

- Nobody knows "the truth" and "all there is to be known" about something. We can only take partial perspectives about that 'something' – and, the more different the perspectives we get in contact

197

with, the more complete is the image we build about that 'something'. Thus, I am merely giving them more options to consider. I help them make a more appropriate decision by making them *aware* of relevant information.

- Moreover, not only I am perfectly OK if they do make comparisons that might lead to a 'no deal', but I would even encourage those comparisons myself, because I want to make sure that they are 100% *congruent* with the buying decision.

- The reality is that *both* types of comparisons are *accurate* for them. For one to make a proper decision, one has to be true to one self and to consider both of them.

- If that "do not buy" comparison is truly relevant in their life, *they* will bring it up and stick with it - and I will respect that.

- Example – if they don't have money for food, for instance - even if I suggest a favorable comparison when presenting the *price*, I will not push, pressure or "manipulate" them to accept it and to buy my product. Above that, I will ask questions to make sure their common sense is active and they realize all the implications. Why? Because I want them *committed* and *engaged* (especially if they are therapy or coaching clients or if I sell a service that they should operate); because I want them to give me good referrals; because I don't want to go through the hassle of them cancelling the order the next day! But, if they find my offer worthwhile, regardless, then I go ahead and make sure that I **serve** them appropriately.

- This "values comparison" also means that by reducing the amount of *money* that I ask for my product, I only diminish the *value* of the product in the eyes of the prospect – because they will compare it with a lower-value "other-thing" from their experience. That will be a dis-service to them, because they will assign less importance to my product and, as a result, they will not make proper use of it.

  - However, I don't want to make false generalizations. Obviously, there will be specific situations where money is really an issue for the client, although they value your offer. That's when your creativity, your reframing and negotiations skills will come to play, so to be able to discount your offer without diminishing its value.

  o At this point, they either pull out their credit card and beg me to take their money (so they could get the *solution*) or they decline the exchange.

Next, I will explain some of the alternatives we have if they decline the exchange. Please understand that this is NOT "handling objections". "Objections" are to be addressed BEFORE they are articulated (See Chapter 22 "About Handling Objections"). So, look at the considerations below and find ways to proactively *address them* **inside** of the *experience* you give them, instead of waiting until the "objection" is expressed.

The proper moment to address those issues is BEFORE they even show up.

If They Refuse My Offer

If they *refuse* my offer, there are two possibilities:

- **One – they found *NO value* in my *offer*;** the *experience* I gave them rose no notable *good feelings* in the prospect. This can mean:

  ○ Either **the *experience* that I gave to them wasn't powerful enough**. Maybe they didn't engage with it. Maybe I wasn't *present*. Maybe I became "needy". Depending on the circumstances, I may or may not suggest another experience. There's no sense in asking for *referrals*. Even if they give me someone's name, it will be a low-quality referral, because they didn't recognize value in my solution.

  ○ Or, **they *paid attention* and found my *offer*, indeed, of no relevance for them**, so I have no business insisting. If I was elegant during the interaction and I developed a *connection* with the prospect, I may ask for *referrals* – because they admit that my *solution* may be *valuable* for some people, although not *for them*.

- **Two – they see *SOME value* for *them* in my *offer* and in my *solution*, but they find it too expensive.** There are two alternatives here; their thinking may go along these lines:

o "too expensive in rapport with what I am willing to spend/ with the resources I actually have"

- That only means that the value they assigned to my solution (in other words, how they feel about it) is less than the value of 'other things' against which that they compared my solution. The pleasure brought by my solution is not higher than the pleasure brought about by the 'other thing' with which they compared it. The options I have now are:

  - I either I take responsibility for the weakness of the experience I gave and offer another experience (if I truly believe that they might accept that).

  - Or, I will ask 'against what' are they comparing that money? I will *ask for permission* to give them another perspective and – after I receive their permission – I bring up yet other comparisons, factual from their life – things on which they are already spending money, that they didn't think at, things which bring them a lower satisfaction (or perhaps even pain) than my solution. See also above, the part where I talked about suggesting value comparisons ahead of time.

o "too expensive in rapport with similar products on the market", as in:

- "I can get same value for less money" – "I can buy something similar with less money (i.e., giving away less value)"

- "I can get more value for the same money" – "I get more value spending this money on something else"

■ Obviously, the question here is "what 'other value' are they comparing your offer with, and to what extent that comparison is valid. If you have a good rapport and connection with them and if you ask and obtain their permission, they may engage in a conversation with you and discuss those details (i.e., how your product will bring more value).

■ I hope you already know to refrain from denigrating the 'other value', because it will turn against you. Why? If they brought it up, most probably they have already a 'belief' about it. Usually, what people believe it's what they hold to be "the truth". When you attack people's "truths", you're attacking their own identity. That can never go well...

■ Thus, if you want to have a real chance for them to try on the perspective you propose (i.e., in which your product is more valuable than their comparison), then they need to continue to feel *safe and secure*, free to take their own decision without any concern that they would be 'pressured' in any way. In order to congruently convey that, you need to remain *present, mindful, detached* of any need of "making them buy". When you ARE this way, then you'll be congruent and they will *feel* it and will trust you. They will feel ok to 'dance' with you through the options you suggest as possibilities.

- If you bring any 'force', 'need' or 'attachment to the outcome' in this dynamics, they will close down and will shut off... they will bring up their barriers; you'll be talking but they will not listen to you.

- I believe that you also need to drop the popular "don't take no for an answer" slogan... instead, be genuinely curious if, indeed, that other product might be more valuable for *this particular* prospect – and, if it really proves to be so, be ready to admit that and stop selling your thing; this will entirely distance you from the large mass of "salespersons" and the prospect will recommend you to their friends (should they need what you have, that is).

  o Note – I said "I ask for permission [to bring another perspective to the table]". Why? Because without their *overt* permission, everything I say after they said *no* will go unnoticed by them, just by their ears - they will not listen to me, unless they commit to listening.

    - There is an old German proverb that says: "Never give advice unless asked." Them giving you permission for that advise is the second best.

However, I am reminding you that **The proper moment to offer those perspectives is DURING the experience of the solution that you give them,** rather than AFTER they told you that it's not valuable to them. Do your best to prime their mind about these possible ramifications as part of your "presentation" or "sample".

To sum up the guidelines:

- Personal preparation

- Offer a Connection

- Offer an experience of your solution

- Give them a real experience that they can feel

- Make an offer for an exchange of value

Remember, these are not "linear" steps. They are organic loops that blend one in each other.

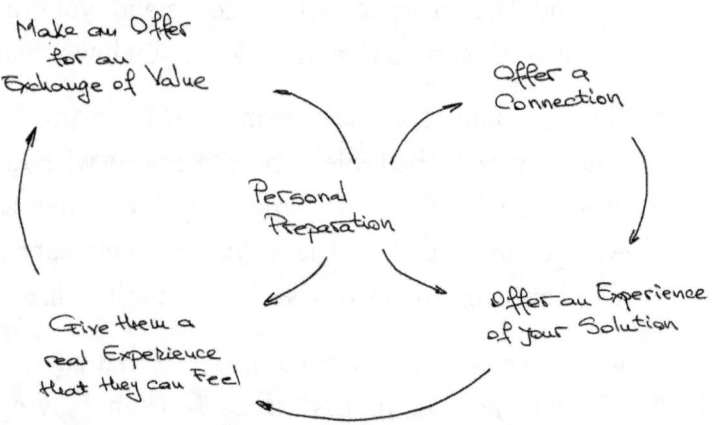

CHAPTER 27:

Prospecting H2H

"I want you to know that there are no colors in the real world, there are no fragrances in the real world, that there's no beauty and there's no ugliness. Out there, beyond the limits of our perceptual apparatus, is the erratically ambiguous and ceaselessly flowing quantum soup. And we're almost like magicians in that in the very act of perception, we take that quantum soup and we convert it into the experience of material reality in our ordinary everyday waking state of consciousness."
Sir John Eccles, Nobel prize in Physiology or Medicine, 1963

I asked salespersons what do they consider to be their biggest challenges in their work. The top-two places were taken by "asking for money" and "prospecting/ making appointments".

Up until here I discussed about the "money" challenge - I uncovered the underground misunderstandings that generate it and I showed you ways of *being* so to "play" with it properly and harmoniously.

Let's talk a bit about *prospecting* and *making appointments*. In other words, how to *stimulate* people to talk to you.

Please note that I didn't use the term "convince" or "persuade" or "get" [as in "*get* people to talk to you"]. I did that in purpose and I encourage you to remove those words from your vocabulary, too. The words that we use are important, since semantics guide and direct our thinking, feelings and behaviors. Words are not "just words". They carry with them *meanings*.

Think of this for a moment....

Surgeons don't "cut your flesh", they "make an incision". It's the same thing, and yet, it is not.

The Problem with Prospecting

When you start your day thinking "I **need** to *convince* somebody to talk to me", that's a very weak and disempowering attitude to have. It puts you on the *victim* position and on a "needy" attitude, which implies that you will "impose", "force" or "make" someone to do something that they don't necessarily want to. It's like preparing for going to war... Moreover, it is highly repellent for your prospects, because they will *sense* your attitude.

No wonder you feel anxious about it and no wonder no one wants to even listen to your greeting and they hung up the phone on you.

You can quickly see how the first thing you can do to increase your chances for having more appointments is to work a bit on the *meanings* that this activity has for you. As long as you see this as a chore where you "get people to do something **for** you" (as in "accept the appointment so *you* can make a presentation"), you will experience difficulties and frustration.

I believe that most "problems" come from the wording itself: "making appointments", "prospecting"... There are a bunch of heavy "meanings" hidden in those words:

- "make" – implies intensity, firmness and stress, the use of force, that you coerce, dominate or overpower somebody or something and you force it to behave as you wish. It unconsciously puts you into a position where you should show strength and determination over someone else. People dislike being abused, you know...

- "appointments" – exudes something official and formal, where the participants' roles are clearly determined (you are selling something to them and they are buying), implies a *decision* to be made, *commitments* to be taken, *contracts* to be signed, and so forth...

  - It also induces in your mind the notion of "numbers": you need "multiple appointments". This idea weakens your ability to *connect* with the person you're talking to *in this moment*, because your attention will involuntarily run towards making "many more" appointments. You lose the individuality, the distinctiveness of *this* conversation you carry *right now*; it becomes "one of the many" and the other person will sense that.

- "prospecting" – it actually means "exploring", but in the sales literature it is defined as "search for potential customers", "find qualified people", "opening a business relationship", "obtaining the commitment for appointment", "funnel for clients", etc. Same as above, it's a very formal, rigid and outcome oriented type of activity.

In other words, there's little elegance and compassion in this set of meanings. And, just the same as *you* sense the attitudes of others when they talk to you, others will sense those attitudes in you, also, when you talk to them.

Most sales authors talk heavily about prospecting tricks, tactics and strategies, making it all "about the salesperson and their outcome"; yes, indeed, at the end, to sweeten their message a bit, they say "salesmanship is about creating relationships"... I find this hypocritical and lacking integrity. Why? Well, how would *you* like for someone to "tactically trick" you into a relationship?

A relationship can only be *allowed* to emerge when the partners feel *safe and secure* with each other, when there is *trust* between them and *freedom of choice.*

Think of this for a moment....

When somebody comes to you with the attitude of "making" you do something, how do you feel? Do you feel like doing it?

What happens when someone really wants to "make" you laugh? Are they funny at all to you?

What happens when someone comes to you, highly energetic, loud and pushy, insisting to "create a relationship" with you and they are not taking 'no' for an answer? On top of that, you know for a fact that they are doing that *only* because they want something **from** you? How is that making you feel about them?

What do you think they should do differently, in order to *allow* for you to accept their request?

Possible Solutions to Prospecting

First of all, since "neediness" stinks, let go of it. Instead, adopt a *playful* attitude. It's vital. When you're "needy", you make the activity "*about you*", and that's repellent. Instead, make it "*about them*"; direct your entire *attention* onto *them* and on what *they* want, while having "zero expectations" for them to say *yes* to you.

Yes, I know, it sounds a bit counter-intuitive and it may feel a bit peculiar at the beginning. However, by not being attached to the outcome you actually show respect for the client and they will sense that. As you embrace this paradox, you'll transcend the alternatives and it will become natural for you.

Secondly, I showed that words like "prospecting" or "making appointments" are loaded with disempowering implicit meanings which will have a negative influence on how the salesperson thinks, feels and ultimately behaves in regards to this activity. That's why I suggest using a different concept, that could empower you more. Try different alternatives and notice how they make you feel. If they help, keep using them. If they don't, try something else. Use different words, with a more "human" connotation, rather than a "corporatist" one, so that will eventually help you *connect* more easily with your prospects.

For instance, I found that successful salespersons use terms such "offer a connection", "break the ice" (so-so), "offer a relationship", "facilitate a connection" (as opposed to "making it happen"), "find friends to play with", and so forth. You can note that these terms do *not* suppose any *force* or *pressure* or any implication that the process of "creating relationship" is under the control of the salesperson and the prospect has no say in this.

If you keep hearing the word "prospecting" in your sales meetings and you cannot distance yourself from it, understand that 'to prospect' means 'to explore'. 'Exploration' implies a sense of curiosity, unexpectedness, discovery of 'what is' (rather than changing it or imposing on it), even 'have fun' with that. The activity, in this sense, is intrinsically motivating, there's no end result that you are running towards and that you "have to" achieve. You are *present* and *connected* with the object of your *exploration* (that is, with your prospect). You are genuinely *allowing* them to make whatever decision they see fit (wanting or not wanting to meet you). You are only setting the conditions to facilitate for them to say "yes" to you, but you are entirely candid and impartial about their decision.

Offer a relationship

'Prospecting' is, indeed, about starting a relationship, but it's *not* a linear process as some authors and sales managers want you to believe. A relationship cannot be "built" the same as you'd build a house. It's an organic process, more like planting a tree - there's no way of telling which way it will go. And the more you force it towards a specific direction, the more resistance the other party will exhibit and the more it will go astray.

A relationship is like a friendship, none of them are possible without *trust*. Trust is not something that you would *ask* from someone, but you *gain* it from someone. To have *their* trust, you need to give them *your trust* first.

How do you give your trust to someone? You show them your *vulnerability*, your *authenticity*, you offer them your friendship, you respect them, you accept with impartiality their decisions (including the one of meeting you or not), you accept them for who they are, you do your best to *understand* them as a human being (i.e., not only as a means to an end, to the wanted *business relationship*).

Prospecting as selling

Look at *prospecting* as an act of *selling*, in and of itself. What's the *exchange of value* here?

Make *prospecting* "about *them*" and "what value *they* receive", instead of "about *you*" and the appointment *you* want to set, for your convenience.

What would constitute *value* for your prospect, in your offer, so that they would accept to meet you? Use the Heart to Heart (H2H) Selling guidelines (Chapter 26 "H2H Selling major guidelines") to *sell* the meeting to your prospect.

The *value* you ask of them is the time, energy and risk of meeting with a potentially "time-wasting" or "annoying" person. What **experience** can you give them *right now*, on the phone, so they could *feel* that meeting with you will be worthwhile for them?

I'm not saying "what promises you can make" or "what tactics you can employ" to "make them believe" that! I am talking about a *real experience* that they can *feel* for themselves, so they can evaluate the *value*, right here, right now.

What gift can you give them, that's valuable to them?

How about your *presence*, as a start?

Example...

Let's say you sell a specific *solution* to a *problem* with which some businesses confront.

A *solution* presupposes the existence of a *problem*, of course. "*Solution*" doesn't exist in and of itself, it comes to life *only* when a correspondent *problem* is admitted upon.

This means that you need to direct the conversation towards the *existence of the problem* to which you have a *solution*. Even more, they need to *admit*, to *recognize* that the *problem* exists for them and that they would value a *solution*. In a basic and schematic form, it goes like this:

- Do you experience this Problem?
- Do you want a Solution?
- Do you want a Solution Now?

Tad James suggests a great opening question, which does all of these things at once:

"We have a *solution* to [such-and-such *problem*]. Are you interested in that, **or not**?"

Thus, the prospect has to think if they have or not that particular *problem*, he has to think about the existence of a *solution* and – in order to weigh his level of interest for it - he has to think about how his business would work like with and without that *solution*.

You can imagine another wording, to your liking, keeping in mind the points that it needs to touch.

Moreover, at all times, remember that your purpose (in selling anything, including this 'appointment') is *not* to "make a sale", but to "offer a fair exchange of value". You offer your 'presence', your 'relationship' and the 'possibility of a *solution*'; in return, you ask for their 'time, energy and risk' (risk of wasting time, of possible "hard sell", etc.). Any hint of pressure, frustration or disrespect from your side will tell them that they should not trust you. So, maintain your state of *presence, playfulness* and *innocence* at all times. It's your most precious "weapon".

Remember to Be Playful

Think of this for a moment...

Many times when I am approached by a salesperson, either by phone or in person, I note that they hold quite a rigid and official attitude. They talk to me with a slight (but obvious) superiority, with authority, a bit "official", with a firm and steady voice, just as if they have "high status" and I have a "lower status"... The feeling I have is that they want to "keep me in a short leash". If I make a comment that deviates them from the course *they* want for the conversation, they treat it with derision or pretend to 'not understand' what I mean. They quickly turn back to their purpose for the conversation with the attitude of "you're wasting my time here".

There's no *playfulness* in this approach, they are "armored up" hiding any sign of vulnerability and their attitude does not make me feel *safe and secure* in their presence, nor appreciated as a human being (only, perhaps, as a potential buyer).

Note: I warned you that this is *not* a book about tactics and strategies to "make" people do whatever you tell them to do. This is a book about **transformation**, about how to **be** the *salesperson* that people trust and respect and want to do business with.

***

I have some bad news, so to speak. I don't want to imply that *prospecting* the way I suggest will be easy for you and that things will miraculously turn around overnight. They might or they might not. Even if you were to be in the perfect state of playfulness and presence, you are still working against a cultural meme that says "all salespersons are imposing on people's lives and if you agree to meet one, you'll have a hard time getting him to leave you alone". Your "colleagues" in the last 50-70 years systematically created this image with their obtrusive and deceiving behavior (not *all*, of course, but most of them). General population's level of trust in salespersons is quite low these days and *trust* is the imperative ingredient in people's relationships. You'll need to encourage their trust in you, and this is a process that requires gentleness, patience and compassion.

The good news is that people **crave** relationships. We are social creatures and we *need* to have friends. That's why, when you show up in a trustworthy way, *present* and you consistently prove yourself to be honest and true, without any hint of imposing or pressuring, people will *want* to be near you and do business with you. They will *want* to help you out.

Compose Yourself

I suggest a bit of *personal preparation* before starting the activity of *prospecting*:

- Find a quiet place and allow yourself to become *present*. Your purpose for doing this is only to *slow down* and *connect* with *yourself*. For how to do it, you can inspire from the other examples in the book or from the exercises on my website (http://www.hearttoheartselling.com/mindfulness.html).

- When you feel quiet and present, evoke the feeling of *having a connection* with your prospect. How would it feel like to talk to a stranger and to become *connected* and *present* with them, as if you were old friends? Don't "force" the feeling, but only evoke it, allow it to emerge. Curiously enough, it may feel different than how you probably assumed. This is the state in which you want both of you to be.

- As that state emerges, enjoy it for a few minutes, rehearse it and memorize it.

- Then, break state, remain *present* and continue with your day. Start doing whatever it is you need to do, while remaining *present* and allowing that evoked feeling to subliminally influence your behavior. Trust that it will.

Think of this for a moment....

Have you ever been selling something to someone and your connection was that high, that the prospect helped you in your selling? They told you what to say or not to say, so that they could buy your product from you?

Or, maybe you were the prospect and you liked the salesperson so much, that you told *them* how to direct the conversation, so that you would end up buying their product?

A good way to facilitate for them to stop judging you through the meme of the cultural stereotype is to facilitate for them to *become present in the moment.* On the Chapter 17 "About Presence" I suggested a few ways to do that.

Note – It's not really possible for me to write here specific prospecting examples per ALL industries. In this Chapter I wanted only to give you the basic *principles* on which to build your own way of *being* an effective *prospecting salesperson.* In the future I will publish approaches for various industries and for day-to-day life applications, like friendship, romantic relationships or parenting – because *everything* is *selling*, isn't it?

CHAPTER 28:

Conclusion and Benefits of H2H Selling

I showed you that:

Selling means *serving* and *offering an exchange of value.*

Selling does not imply "convincing", "persuasion", "manipulation" or "deceiving".

Selling by *giving an experience* is the most effective way for the prospect to recognize *value* in your *offer* and to own their buying decision.

Selling and Buying are distinct processes. Selling is what the salesperson does, and Buying is what the client does. Selling takes place even if the client decides to *not buy.*

Selling implies the existence of a *relationship* between the salesperson and the prospect. Thus, *connection* and *presence* are of the essence. The salesperson is to "forget" and let go of their neediness and make the process *about the client,* so to facilitate that *relationship* to emerge.

When your actions are guided by your "set, then forgotten" *intention,* free of neediness or attachment to the outcome, while directing your entire *attention* onto your prospect, you increase the quality of your *influence.* The prospect will feel *safe and secure* and they can allow themselves to *become present* and *aware* of the *value* of your *offer.*

The prospect's sales reluctance is generally ignited and fueled by the salesperson's attitude of "I want something **from** you".

- When your attitude changes to "I want something **for** you", you bring no 'forcing' to the interaction; the prospect can relax, feel safe and secure in your presence and accept to *play* and *dance* with you.

- To want something **for** them means *to be of service.*

- *To be of service* means to offer something of *value*, in a way that they can appreciate.

- That means you maintain equanimity and "noble indifference" in regards to their chosen response to our *offer.*

- Selling is not about the result of this *offering.* Selling **is** the *offering.*

People always want more value in their lives, it's in the human nature. If they decline a proposed *exchange*, it's only because they don't recognize *receiving* enough *value* from it or because their focus misguides them. It's not about the *money.* And, certainly, it's not about *you.*

Selling with a *playful* attitude is the best way to *engage* prospects into an *experience.*

Prospecting with a *playful* attitude is the best way to 'offer a connection'.

Selling does not refer strictly to the economical transactions. We may say that Selling is just another name for Influence. *Selling* is present in every aspect of life, from friendships to romantic relationships to parenting. When approaching these interactions, too, from a *Heart to Heart* perspective, of *serving* and *exchange of value*, only good things can happen.

You can enjoy and have fun Influencing from the Heart!

Glossary of Terms

"If you wish to converse with me, define your terms."
Voltaire

For the sake of brevity and to minimize misunderstandings, allow me to briefly comment on a few practical terms. These are useful **distinctions** about how I am using those concepts in the context of Heart to Heart Selling. You will make use of them more effectively when you grasp their meaning the way I intended. Please keep in mind that I am *not* implying that these are the *mainstream* definitions. They only represent my own understandings of those terms and the way they apply to the "Heart to Heart Selling" model.

(I arranged them in alphabetical order, for easiness in finding the one you need to review)

Asking for permission – it's a great way for me to obtain the listener's *commitment for listening* to me, for them giving me their attention and for engaging with my 'sales presentation' or 'sample of my solution'.

Attention – when I have someone's *attention*, they are *in the present moment, connected* with me, focusing on me or on a common subject. It's a key element – until I have someone's *attention*, I have no true conversation, because they are *elsewhere*. They are not thinking of me, so I actually carry a monologue, not a conversation. My words will make no impact on their experience of reality.

Closing vs Agreement – *closing* is the old-school term that defines the "phase" where the salesperson employs all sorts of techniques in order to "make" the client sign the contract. Although some people may say that "a word is just a word", I see this term as inappropriate and disempowering, especially when *agreement* implies that both parties *mutually agreed* about the exchange (not that one party *made* the other one to agree). *Agreement* presupposes *opening a relationship* between me and the client.

Congruent vs Incongruent –

- When I am *congruent,* all of my values, thoughts, feelings and behaviors are oriented in the same direction. When I am doing something *congruently,* my *internal representations* (i.e., how and what I am thinking *about* that 'doing') are also aligned with that *behavior.* There is *no conflict* between what I am doing on the *outside* and what's happening on my *inside* world of thoughts and feelings.

- When I act *incongruently,* I am doing a certain action or behavior, but my beliefs and values are in *conflict* with that action. I may act bravely, but inside I am telling to myself that I shouldn't do this or I imagine myself failing. My beliefs and values are *not aligned* with my behavior, and this makes me feel awkward. The person watching me will sense that *incongruity* and their trust in me will start to erode.

Connection – I believe that we are all already *connected,* but we are not aware of this connection because we think ourselves out of it – just like, right now, you are not aware of your left little toe... but you are becoming aware of it as you put your attention on it.

When I put aside my Ego and its "needy" stories and I just *slow down* to really see, hear and feel the other person, I am allowing myself to become *aware* of the *existing* connection between us. All that I need to do is 'nothing' (that is, 'stop doing' and just pay attention). Connection "happens" all by itself when two people are *present,* focusing on each other or on the same thing.

Convincing and **Persuasion** – are conscious, overt methods of motivating and leading someone to a *specific* conclusion or action (that I want them to adopt). I am mainly using logical arguments, presenting the benefits of *yes* and the loses of *no.* The purpose is to "make" people choose *the one conclusion* that I want them to choose. (In a sense, *convincing* is blunt and direct, using rational arguments, while *persuasion* is a bit more "sneaky", using "baits", enticements, lures and even threats and decoys)

- For instance, bringing arguments to the freshly smoke-free person that one cigarette cannot do any harm and that nobody will know, that's *convincing.*

- Did you know that "convince" comes from the Latin "convincere", meaning *"to prove wrong"*, *"to conquer"*? How enjoyable does this sound to you?

Deceiving – I am deceiving someone when I deliberately tell things that *I know for a fact* they are untrue or deliberately hide things that are true, in order to *directly* conduce someone into making a decision to my advantage, and to their disadvantage.

We also need to consider that people "lie" all the time, simply because "the truth" is a fantasy. Even saying to somebody "the time is 2 o'clock" may raise philosophical questions of credibility or truthfulness. "To lie" or "to not lie" it's an old puzzle, a false dichotomy which – in my opinion – finds its solution on a higher perspective that reconciles both alternatives (if you still cling on the idea of the "absolute truth", consider the Santa Claus story you tell to your kids).

The way I see it, the difference stands in the **intention,** in the *purpose* with which I tell that "lie" to my prospect and in the *attitude* that I hold. In playing, we aim to "deceive" and to "outwit" our opponents all the time as part of the game, but never with the intention to hurt them and only for as long as the interaction remains enjoyable for all (the way each one of us experiences it).

Here there are some thoughts to consider:

- What do I want to create through that statement?

    o Do I tell a "false" story with the purpose of making a point, of setting up the frames for the conversation, of facilitating an experience, or

    o Am I saying it with the clear purpose of altering and disguising the experience itself, so that what I show them now [about my product] is something different than what they will experience after they purchased the product?

        ▪ Saying "I did this presentation a hundred times and I know you'll enjoy it" (when I only did it twenty times and I have no way of knowing if they will enjoy it or not) it's not necessarily deceiving, because the intention of the statement is to prime the prospect's mind for an enjoyable experience.

        ▪ Hiding the fact that the gas tank is perforated (when selling my old car) is deceiving, because I *need* them to buy the car and,

222

having known the fact, the prospect would not buy it.

■ Selling a cruise assuring the client that it's "free", while knowing that there are lots of hidden charges and fees to cover, that's deceiving.

- What's the intention of my statement? Is it "to get something from them" or "to give something for them"?

- Is my attitude one of playfulness, enjoying the moment, the interaction or is one of chasing or forcing the favorable outcome that I want for me?

    o Think again of the Santa Claus stories we tell to our children. What's your intention and attitude when you say those stories? That's where the difference stands.

- Where is my *attention*? Is it in the flowing of the interaction or on the outcome that I want?

- It is also a matter of *values* that I have.

Ego – Ego (without becoming too technical or philosophical) it's part of my Conscious Thinking and it's represented by the stories I tell myself about who I am, what I should do, or not do, what to like or dislike, etc. Ego builds these stories, but I am not necessarily aware of what they actually say. However, they dictate my decisions, my thinking and my behaviors. Those stories are many and intricate, more of less coherent among them, and that's why Ego doesn't like *change* – because any little *change* in one story will require changes in many other stories, just to keep up the *relative coherence* among them.

○ Another issue with the Ego is that it always judges what happens *now* by comparing it with something else that happened in the *past*. That's why, when people label me as a 'salesperson', they bring their past experiences to judge me. They don't judge me for who I am *now* or for what I am doing *now*. They judge me from the lenses of what happened to them in the *past*. They are not talking to me, but to that salesperson from their past. If it happens that they had a pleasant past experience, then I have a chance that they will listen to me. But if they had an unpleasant experience, then they will defensively close down, because the voice from their past is "trustworthy" (since it's coming from within). To stop that, I need to bring them *in the now*, for them to be *present* with me, because Ego has no room in the *present moment*. We talked about how to do that, because is crucial for a real conversation to even take place (see Chapter 17 "About Presence")

Engagement – presupposes their *attention* and their *willingness to play* with me and to partake in the process, full heartedly. Hint: people *play* only with partners they *trust* and feel *safe and secure* with; more importantly, with partners who *don't carry a need to win.*

Enthusiasm – etymologically speaking, it means "inspired by gods". Thus, for me, "having enthusiasm" means "being *connected* with *what is, in the present moment*". It has nothing to do with the popular understanding that I should be extrovert, pumped-up or loud.

Exchange of Value – the *value* inside of a community grows only when it is *exchanged* among its members.

Extrinsic vs Intrinsic motivation –

- *extrinsic motivation* means that my reward is what I get out of the activity I am doing (for a sales interaction it may be the commission, the recognition, etc.).

- *intrinsic motivation* means that I find my pleasure and satisfaction just from engaging in that activity (e.g., the sales interaction), regardless of the result of it. I get my 'confirmation' just from connecting with that prospect. If they become a client, that's a bonus.

  o I still have the *intention* for reaching an *agreement* and I am still *influencing/ nudging* the conversation towards an *agreement*, but only indirectly; during the interaction with the prospect, that's secondary. What's primary? It's my focus on *connecting* and *serving* them, to the best of my abilities, while *letting go of the need* for their acceptance.

- For instance, an artist (e.g., a singer) finds her satisfaction and reward in the act of singing, in and of itself. It's true, she sings for the public and she wants the public to enjoy her art. However, during the singing, she is *lost* in that singing, she is *present*, finding her enjoyment in the act of singing. She forgot about the money, about the problems with her boyfriend or about the quarrel with her manager. She *is in the flow* with the process of singing. In those moments, there is *no end result* in her preoccupations. The singing is not merely a means to an end, it *is* her end result.

- I can '*want* something to happen' (i.e., I may 'have an

intention'), even while acting out of intrinsic motivation. It's only when I *'need* that something to happen', that my motivation turns into extrinsic.

o How do I know that my *wanted intention* turned into *need*? I take note of how I would feel if I were to *not* get the result: if I feel pain, disappointment, hurt, anger, etc., this it's a sign I became *needy*.

▪ Can you *want* something without *needing* it?

Forcing – this term, for me, is more about the *internal attitude* of the salesperson, rather than the methods they employ. In using this term, I want to emphasize that the salesperson carries a *need* for a *specific outcome* and that this *neediness* transpires in the way the frustrated salesperson acts and talks, making the entire process tense and unpleasant. The salesperson's attitude is one of "I won't take 'no' for an answer, I'm not letting you off the hook, I will look for any clues that I can use to control your responses."

• *influence* and *forcing* refer mainly to *attitudes* and sit at the extremities of the "neediness" spectrum – the *need* for a *specific* end result, that is. A metaphor that comes to mind is that of *invitation vs pushing*. The moment one loses one's *equanimity* about the end result, one *stops influencing* and *starts forcing*.

• *Convincing, persuasion* and *manipulation* generally imply the *need* for a *specific* end result. However, I could employ the **same** *tools* and *techniques* without "neediness". That means, the difference that makes the difference in their usage is the *intention* I have. It is the *forcing* (born out of *neediness* for one and only result) which makes them "bad smelling". When I let go of the need for a *specific* end result and I become *impartial* about it, I am now *influencing*, although I am using the very *same tools.*

 o The tricky part is that this distinction cannot be "proven" by an outside observer; they may try to 'mind read' me, but only I know the truth.

Giving an *experience* of my *solution* – ... as opposed to just explaining or offering a mere intellectual understanding of that *solution...*

- However, even when I am only *describing* that solution to the client, that conversation can become an *experience* for them when they *engage* and *pay attention, present* and *connected.* That's the power of storytelling.

Go First – Before meeting my client, I stop for a moment and *become present.* I *evoke* the feeling I'd like my prospect to feel at the end of the *experience* I'm just about to give them. I *feel that now* and maintain that feeling during my conversation. I *feel now the way I want them to feel* at the end. If I want them to like me (for instance), I like them first - but not as an "equation", not with the "expectation" or "entitlement" that they should respond in a similar way. This attitude will turn everything you do into a "tactic" and will arise in me the "neediness". Since I want the "real thing" from them (that is, I want them to like me "for real"), that means that I have to *unconditionally* give them "the real" thing first.

Golden Rule – on its 'active' interpretation: "Treat others as you would like others to treat you". To realize how to sell harmoniously, I put myself in the shoes of my prospect and I take note: in which way I would like somebody to sell to me?

- I'll adapt it for selling: "*Make an offer* to others as you would like others to sell to you, *while asking for permission and respecting their freedom* to accept your offer or not."

- Why "asking for permission?" Because everybody else is _not_ like you. Suppose I am talking to a lady and I would like to be kissed by her. This doesn't mean that I should assume that she would also like to be kissed by me and it's ok for me to go ahead and kiss her! However, I could offer her that, I could ask permission for that, while holding my equanimity and non-attachment in regards to her response [this is just a metaphor...].

High quality action – it happens when I am *present, engaged* and *playing*. It's about "being in the *flow*". I set an *intention* (i.e., to *serve* this prospect) and then I "forget" about it. I focus entirely on connecting with what I do, while allowing that *intention* to only *indirectly* affect my behavior.

Influence – it's a natural phenomenon that happens spontaneously and continuously. It's like gravity: it simply exists and we all use it. We are all influencing each other all the time, more or less deliberately. It's something no one can escape. It usually happens randomly, but I can *nudge it towards* a certain outcome by recognizing and using the natural patterns. I can put things in motion, with the intention for them to go to a certain place, but I don't try to control the outcome.

Influence presupposes a harmonious flow, easiness and patience. *Influence* implies that the outcome is *not needed* or *forced*, but only *intended*. Many outcomes are *possible and allowed*. The "influencee" has freedom of choice, at all levels. The "influencer" is entirely *candid* and *indifferent* about "target's" decision. It's like *play* – in a genuine *play*, the players want to win, but they are OK if they don't; the fun comes from the challenge, from the unknown. If they knew for a fact who will win (that some particular outcome will happen with 100% certainty, that is), there will be no more pleasure in the game... My attitude, as a salesperson, is one of "I am letting you go, so you could come back on your own – or not."

- For instance, when I put a seed in the ground and I water it, is *influence.*

- If I smoke, or even if I put my pack of cigarettes on the table, in front of a person who just quit smoking, is *influence.* The other person continues to have total *freedom of choice.*

  - However, by doing that, I disregard The Golden Rule (considering that I wouldn't like others to do that to me);

- Did you know that "influence" comes from Latin "influere", composed of "in" and "fluere" (meaning "flow")?. So, "to influence" means *"to be in the flow"*

Let go of the *need* (for a particular outcome) – I refrain from becoming attached to the outcome. As Steve Chandler put it: "needy is creepy". I maintain the *want*, but in a detached way.

Low quality action – That's happening when I use the *present moment* only as a *means to an end*. It's when I carry the attitude of "I'll be happy when..." (e.g., "I'll be happy when they buy"). That's a *low quality of mind*, conducive to a *low quality of behavior*.

Making an *offer* – I propose an *exchange of value* for acceptance or non-acceptance, I make it available. I have *no attachment* for a particular answer from the prospect. My attitude is one of equanimity and innocence.

Manipulation – in its foul meaning, it's about getting someone to take a *certain* action by tapping into their *weak* points, into their feelings of fear, shame, guilt, and so forth.

- For instance, if I tell to that guy who just quit smoking that he is not man enough if he cannot smoke a cigarette without being afraid of relapsing into smoking again – that's manipulation.

- If I distract the client who just pointed out an *uncomfortable* detail, by asking "smoke screen" questions, is manipulation.

Money – it's a representation of *value* - it is not *value*, in and of itself. We use *money* in order to "measure" a certain *value* and to "compare" it with some other *value*. *Money* is for *value* what *inches* are for *length*.

Neediness – appears when I am holding a *need* for a *specific outcome* from that interaction. That makes me inflexible, uncreative and unattractive.

Play – it's a physical or mental activity that has no purpose or objective outside of pure enjoyment or amusement. *Play* is not a means to an end. Although the players would *like* to win the game (as a "justification", an "excuse" for the activity itself, so to avoid making the 'enjoyment' too conscious of a purpose), for all they know they already won; their reward is *now*, in the *playing*, in and of itself. They don't have a *need* to win the actual game, which makes it even more probable that they *will* win, paradoxically.

- In contrast, some people consider that their reward lies in the *end result* of the process: if they win, *then* they will feel good. For them, the *future* is more important than what's happening *now*. They only use the *present* as a means to an *end*, which is always in the *future*, somewhere.

230

Presence, Flow, Mindfulness, Being *present* **in the** *moment* – Usually, we allow our *minds* to spontaneously carry us into the *past* or into the *future*, making us feel *regrets* or *fears*. But when we pay attention to what happens *right now*, we become *present to the moment*.

When I am *present*, I have all of my *attention, creativity* and *thinking* focused on the person I am talking to. I am aware and alert. Everything I *think*, *feel* and *do* is only aimed towards understanding this person. I let go and put aside all of my *regrets* about the *past* and all of my *anxieties* and *desires* about the *future*. In the entire world there's only me and this person I am talking to *right now*.

Problem – Generally speaking, there are two types of 'problems':

1. A person fell into a lower condition than their 'normality' and they want to recover back to where they were;

2. A person feels dissatisfied with their current condition and they want more, they want an advancement.

We may say that solving the first type of problem would be "regenerative therapy", and the second type would be "transformative coaching". From a *selling* perspective, just to keep it simple, I will make no distinction between those two types of problems. I will say that when a person sees value in moving from the current state of things to another, when they want a different life experience than the current one, they have a *problem* to which they want a *solution*.

Prospecting – the activity where I find people who have and admit having a *problem* to which they want a solution *now*, from whom I want to receive *permission for giving them an experience of my solution to their problem.*

Safe and Secure - For the prospect to honestly answer my questions and to fully engage with an open mind in the conversation with me, they need to feel *safe and secure* in my presence. For someone to "play" or "dance" with me, they need to feel *safe and secure*. For someone to accept having a *relationship* with me, they need to feel *safe and secure* with me. *Trust* is of the essence. When I am "needy" and I "transpire" having an *ulterior motive*, they cease to feel *safe*. They will stop trusting me and will start second-guessing everything that I do. Their mind closes. They don't listen to me anymore, but to their own judgments in regards to what I say.

Selling – selling is the process where I connect with a person, I note if they admit to having a problem for which they want a solution *now,* I ask for permission and I offer them an experience of my solution to their problem, and – if they find value in my solution – I make a proposal for an exchange of value.

- That is all there is to it. The *buying* decision belongs to them. I have no right to impose my product or service upon their lives, even if I truly believe that it will be "good" for them.

- Selling is like change-work or therapy; as the salesperson, I am asking the client to literally change their world, so that their reality would seamlessly incorporate my product/ service. This means that – at some level - the client should re-align their values. From my experience as a hypnotherapist, the client cannot be forced to change their values, but only influenced, in a mindful and non-attached manner.

- Also, they need to *want* to do it - for the change-work to be a harmonious process. When people are "forced" or "pushed", they often push back. That's why the therapist must maintain its own sense of *presence* and *connection*, remaining un-attached of the outcome, letting go of any "need" of "getting something *from* the client" and focusing only on "wanting something *for* the client". The change happens by "invitation", not by "pushing".

Service vs Servitude –

- Servitude implies that I submitted my power to the client, I am there only to *please* their Ego.

- Service means that I am actively working for the greater good of my client. I am not concerned about their Ego, but only about *serving* and fulfilling the terms of the *agreement* we had made.

Solution – something that will facilitate for them to resolve the *problem* they experience.

Suspect vs Prospect vs Client

- A "suspect" is a person I imagine might need my service or might know somebody who could need it - but I don't know that yet. It is *only a supposition, a possibility to explore*. So, I ask them **if** they have a *problem* or I talk and connect with them, and notice if they mark out having a *problem*.

  o In this sense, a 'suspect' is merely a human being I am offering to connect with [Please leave out the juridical sense, where a 'suspect' implies 'guilty'...].

- A "prospect" is a previous "suspect" who confirmed that they *do* have a *problem* to which they *want* a *solution,* and they want it *now.* They agreed to have an *experience* of my *solution.*

- A "client" is a "prospect" who *agreed* to an *exchange of value*: I give them my *solution,* and they give me the *value* that I want in return (might be *money* as a representation for the *value* I want, or a referral, a learning, an experience, etc.).

Toxic vs Healthy outcome

- *toxic outcome* – appears when my gratification and my personal sense of value is delayed and dependent to the realization of that end result. My motivation for that outcome is *extrinsic* - there's *no joy on doing* the activity; the purpose of the activity is the *end result;*

- *healthy outcome* – appears when my reward and sense of success comes from *doing the activity.* I continue doing it simply because I keep getting a reward each and every second I am doing it. It's like Play: my motivation for that outcome is *intrinsic* – the purpose of the activity lies *in* the activity, in and of itself.

Thank you for reading!

Dear Reader,

I hope you enjoyed the message in **Heart to Heart Selling: Create clients through nurturing connection**. I personally enjoyed writing it and I appreciated it more and more, each time I re-read and edited the text. Some people asked me "Is this really working in real life?" Well, not only that I used these concepts to guide my life for the last 7 years (although on and off, more or less randomly!), but now, having clear distinctions and guidelines in place, I apply them in all walks of life, in all interactions that I have. These are some of the questions that I ask myself: am I present?; am I connected with myself?; is the other person present with me?; do we have a connection?; what's the exchange of value here?; am I attached to the outcome or I am playful?

As a coach, a trainer and an author, I love feedback. My deepest intention is to serve you in becoming a win-win 'deliberate influencer' in your life. So, tell me what you liked in this message, what was useful for you or what do you think it's missing. You may have questions about how to integrate these principles in your life: tell me about it and, if I can help, I'll be glad to. There may even be parts of the book that you didn't like or you don't agree with: I want to hear about that, too. Somebody said "I enjoy being wrong, because that's the only time when I learn something" and I agree with that. I'd love to hear from you and to serve you the best I can. You can write me at info@hearttoheartselling.com and visit me on the web at www.hearttoheartselling.com.

All in all, if you found this message by any means valuable, I want to ask you a favor. Would you be willing to write an honest review of **Heart to Heart Selling**? This way, we encourage other people to – at least – 'Look inside' the book and get a sense if they can make good use of its message or not. If you have the time and the inclination, go to www.amazon.com, login to your account, go to "Your Orders" or "Your Digital Orders" and click on "Write a product review".

Thank you for reading Heart to Heart Selling and for allowing me to connect with you.

Love and Kindness,

Cezar

Research, References and Acknowledgments

This list cannot be comprehensive because I've been influenced and inspired by so many great minds, too many to mention – or even remember - all of them. I apologize in advance if I forgot to mention somebody worthwhile of being mentioned here.

B., Rishan

Awaken through Mindfulness

Bateson, Gregory

Epistemology, Language, Play and the Double Bid

Chandler, Steve

The Joy of Selling

Chandler, Steve and Litvin, Rich

The Prosperous Coach

Cialdini, Robert

Influence, The Psychology of Persuasion

Cohen, Steve

Win the Crowd

Covey, Stephen

The seven habits of highly effective people

Csikszentmihalyi, Mihaly

Flow

Curzan, Anne

TED talk: What makes a word "real"?

Dawson, Roger

The Secrets of Power Negotiating

Dispenza, Joe

Rewiring Your Brain to a New Reality

Dyer, Wayne

The Power of Intention

Fehmi, Les and Robbins, Jim

The Open Focus Brain

Gendlin, Eugene T.

Focusing

Goswami, Amit

The Self-Aware Universe

Groover, Rachael Jayne

Awaken Your Impact

Groover, Rachael Jayne

Power and Presence

Hayes, Steven C.

Get Out of your mind and into your life

Hill, Napoleon

Research, References and Acknowledgments

Selling You

Hogan, Kevin

The Science of Influence

James, Tad

5 Step Sales Process

James, Tad

Using NLP In Business

Johnstone, Keith

Impro - Improvisation and the Theatre

Lao-tzu

Tao Te Ching

Ledochowski, Igor

Mind Bending Language

Ledochowski, Igor

Money In Your Mind

Leonard, Thomas J.

The 28 Laws of Attraction

Lewis, Philip M.

The Discerning Heart, The Developmental Psychology of Robert Keagan

Moine, Donald and Lloyd, Kenneth

Unlimited Selling Power

Pinci, Larry and Glosserman, Phil

Sell the Feeling

Robbins, Anthony

Mastering Influence

Robinson, Ken

TED talk: "Bring on the learning revolution!"

Smart, Jamie

Clarity

Smart, Jamie

Getting Clients Congruently

Sullivan, Wendy and Rees, Judy

Clean Language

Tolle, Eckhart

The Power of Now

Tracy, Brian

Psychology of Selling

Tracy, Brian

Sales Master Academy

Tripp, James

Changework

Tripp, James

Create Instant Change

Tripp, James

Research, References and Acknowledgments

Hypnosis Without Trance

Yahya, Harun

Matter, The Other Name for Illusion

Inspiring ideas and distinctions from:

Hulse, Elliott

Korzybski, Alfred

Morgan, John P.

Sinek, Simon

Watts, Alan